The Official

England Rugby

HEROES

This edition published by SevenOaks in 2015

Carlton Books Limited
20 Mortimer Street
London W1T 3JW

Copyright © Carlton Books Limited 2015

Rugby Football Union. The Red Rose and the words "England Rugby" are official registered trademarks of the Rugby Football Union and are subject to extensive trademark registration worldwide.

RFU Official Licensed Product: The RFU guarantees that all profits from the sale of products and services carrying the Invest in Rugby Mark will be invested into rugby at all levels in England. Englandrugby.com/invest

A CIP catalogue record for this book is available from the British Library.

10 9 8 7 6 5 4 3 2 1

ISBN 978-1-78177-262-1

Project Editor: Matt Lowing
Project Art Editor: Luke Griffin
Picture research: Paul Langan
Editorial: Caroline Curtis and Chris Parker
Designer: Darren Jordan
Production: Maria Petalidou

Printed in Dubai

The Official
England Rugby
HEROES

JULIAN BENNETTS

SEVENOAKS

England captain Martin Johnson and the extra-time hero Jonny Wilkinson both made significant contributions to England's 2003 Rugby World Cup-winning campaign.

CONTENTS

FOREWORD
BILL BEAUMONT

I spent eight years playing for England, years that shaped my entire life.

Barely a day goes by when I am not asked what it was like to play for my country and captain the team. More than that, people want to know what it felt like to win something as momentous as the Grand Slam in 1980, the first time in 23 years we had done so.

It was fantastic, of course, and the fact so many people still remember those days tells me this: if you achieve something playing for England then it will be remembered forever.

Supporters who weren't even born in 1980 talk about what we did that year, and I'm sure the same goes for Will Carling's sides of the early 1990s, or Sir Clive Woodward's wonderful team from 2003.

How we all hope that Stuart Lancaster and Chris Robshaw can reach similar heights when they lead this wonderfully promising and exciting young England side during the Rugby World Cup later this year.

And Stuart himself would be interested in this book, as he is a man who makes a virtue of England's fine rugby history.

The current players know more about their predecessors than any other England side; the stories of Arthur Harrison, James Peters and Cyril Lowe are an inspiration to them.

Their tales, some of them quite remarkable, are included here.

It is an honour for me to be included in a book such as this, as it always is when your record and achievements in the sport are mentioned by others.

I am glad to see so many of my playing colleagues remembered too. Rugby is perhaps the ultimate team sport. It is about both individual inspiration and collective effort.

My memories of playing for my country are proud and vivid. You are aware at the time that it is important, that it matters. You play for something greater than yourself, and the 35 years since that superb day at Murrayfield have brought that home to me more than ever.

You are also aware that it is fleeting. You are a custodian of the shirt, and know you must leave it in a fine condition for the next man and the next generation to reach ever greater heights.

This is the story of the best of those who have worn the England shirt. Those of us in it are honoured to have played our part, and cannot wait for others to add their chapters.

I hope you enjoy it.

A legion of England rugby heroes, including Roger
Uttley, Bill Beaumont and Fran Cotton, Peter Wheeler
and Robin Cowling, look on from below the uprights
in a Five Nations match against Wales in 1977.

INTRODUCTION

One of the first things Stuart Lancaster did when he was appointed England's Head Coach was to invite a series of former players to give presentations to the current squad.

"We were looking into the identity of the England team and what it means to be English and represent this team," he later explained.

"We definitely made a really strong connection with the players from previous eras. We asked them to articulate what it meant to play for England at that time, and also what it means to see England be successful now.

"They were delighted to contribute. What we were looking for were some anchors that can provide traits for what England sides have done in the past and we can say: 'This is what being English is and this is what playing for this team is.'"

In looking to the past, Lancaster was trying to build a stronger future.

The players themselves took it a step further, and formed a Heritage Committee to look into examples of former England players who could provide inspiration to Chris Robshaw, George Ford and the rest. Now, the Arthur Harrison Awards are presented to the team's outstanding performers after every match.

It is named after Lieutenant-Commander Arthur Harrison, winner of two England caps before his death at Zeebrugge on 23 April 1918. For his bravery that day, Harrison was posthumously awarded the Victoria Cross. He is the only English rugby union international to receive such an honour.

For others their battle was lonely and without recognition, but no less inspirational. James Peters's story also had a profound effect on the squad, in particular the Vunipola brothers. The first black man to play for England, Peters made two appearances for the national side in 1907. His story was not a particularly happy one, but it paved the way for the likes of Mako and Billy, and it serves to inspire them even now.

These are just some of the reasons why the history of the England rugby team is so important, to the current side and to fans. When Lancaster asked for the Twickenham dressing rooms to be remodelled, he ensured that there was a board inside England's inner sanctum listing every single international. And above each peg is a list of some of the finest England players in that particular position.

"When we got in there, we could show the players the history wall, the debut board and also behind each player's changing spot were the names of those who had played in their position before," said Lancaster.

"So you get across the point that you are not just playing for your friends and family but also those who have played previously in your position."

Such logic also explains why the last thing the England players see in the Twickenham tunnel before they emerge into the arena are the words "Hundreds before you. Thousands around you. Millions behind you."

This England side feels both the pride and the pressure of being in such illustrious company.

All the players are fully aware of the sacrifices made by many of the men in these pages. Those such as Cyril Lowe who, despite losing a number of years of his rugby career to the First World War, made the most of his astonishing talent. Lowe set a Five Nations try-scoring record that still stands today.

There are men in this book who could inspire the current team in a number of different ways. Brian Moore was one of the proudest men to play for England, his pure aggression leading to a well-deserved nickname of "Pitbull". Yet he knew that victory required more than just physical dominance. Very few other England internationals have attempted to put themselves in the right frame of mind by reading Shakespeare.

Alternatively, they might wish to flick straight to the pages detailing England's three Grand Slams between 1991 and 1995, or the myriad players and coaches who were involved in the 2003 World Cup triumph. More than 20 of them are profiled in this book, including legends of the English game such as Martin Johnson, Jonny Wilkinson and Lawrence Dallaglio.

This book is a link to English rugby's past, the stories included in it highlighting both the pride and the responsibility of playing for your country. At the time of writing there are just under 1,400 men who have played for England since the first international against Scotland in 1871.

Together they form an incredibly strong collective, and the finest of them are listed here. This book attempts to lay out the greatest parts of English rugby history, the characters and narrative that Lancaster feels are so important to the current team.

Each of the men in this book has his name listed in the hallowed walls of the Twickenham changing rooms. They have left their mark. Now we will see if Robshaw, Dan Cole, Ben Youngs and the rest can do the same as the 2015 World Cup comes into view.

One important caveat: there can never be a definitive list of rugby heroes. The list will always need to be updated. Those currently wearing the England shirt will look after it as best they can, and some of them will prove as inspirational as the men before them. And then a new generation will arrive, with new ambitions and new heroes to look up to.

"This is what being English is and this is what playing for this team is," Lancaster said when describing why he had attempted to connect his players to their team's history. This is their history, and now they must add to it.

England's Jeremy Guscott expertly hands off France's Xavier Garbajosa in 1999. The centre's grace and attacking verve could unlock the tightest of defences and helped England to reach a Rugby World Cup in 1991.

As every great captain should, England skipper Chris Robshaw leads by example and can be seen taking the game to South Africa in November 2014.

England Rugby

HEROES

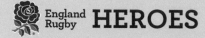
ALFRED ST GEORGE HAMERSLEY

Hamersley played for England in the first ever rugby union international and went on to captain his country before introducing the game to New Zealand and Canada.

Alfred St George Hamersley (pictured middle row, second from the left) left a real legacy in the sport of rugby union – although, if we are being honest, it is one that has cost his own country dear at times.

A talented player who captained England, Hamersley was a solicitor and moved abroad after the end of his playing career, taking the game with him. His travels took him to New Zealand, where he is credited with introducing rugby union to the youth of South Canterbury.

His next stop was Vancouver, Canada, in 1888. A year after his arrival, he was voted President of the British Columbia Rugby Union, a sign of the impact he had made.

His rugby career had started, like so many others, at Marlborough College. A tall, powerful forward who was particularly effective in the scrum, he played in the first international between Scotland and England in Edinburgh. In front of

an attendance of 4,000 at Raeburn Place, Scotland defeated England by one goal and one try to one try.

When England gained revenge the following year at The Oval, Hamersley scored a try. The third game between the sides was drawn and then, in 1874, with Hamersley as captain, England won again.

That was to prove his final game for England as he set about exploring new parts of the world.

Two months after that match, he set sail from Plymouth to Melbourne, and from there travelled to New Zealand. As well as spreading the rugby gospel, Hamersley founded the New Zealand Grand National Steeplechase club.

Some 14 years later he moved to Vancouver, where he is credited with being the country's first solicitor.

In retirement, he returned to England and in 1909 helped form the club that would become Oxford RFC – a final act for the game to which he gave so much.

ENGLAND STATISTICS
March 1871 – February 1874
England appearances: 4
England points: 0

ENGLAND STATISTICS
February 1881 – December 1882
England appearances: 5
England points: 0 – but 3 tries; points were not awarded for tries until the late 1880s

HARRY VASSALL

A fine player, administrator and author on rugby, Harry Vassall helped reinvent the way the game was played and enjoyed a key role in England's early success.

The scorer of the first hat-trick in international rugby union, Harry Vassall (pictured back row, second from the left) dedicated his life to the sport and helped transform it by inventing the role of the modern halfback.

One of the finest figures in Oxford's illustrious rugby heritage, he captained his University to an astonishing 70 matches without defeat, and his success was rewarded with five England appearances from 1881.

He is perhaps best remembered, however, for helping to revolutionize the way the game was played. Alongside team-mate Alan Rotherham, Vassall was integral in realizing that the halfbacks should link both forwards and backs, transforming rugby as a sport. Before this, rugby had been very static. Now it became a far more enjoyable spectacle and drew in the crowds.

Vassall's rugby career began at Marlborough College, and he continued his progression at Oxford where he was awarded a Blue in 1879. The following year, he was appointed Oxford secretary and arranged trials to ensure the best team was chosen and that the outfit was run as professionally as possible.

In 1881 England were due to play Wales at Blackheath, the latter's first ever rugby union international. A space was left free in the English team for someone from Oxford and Vassall – who was completely unknown to the Welsh – filled it.

The selection was a resounding success, and Vassall became the first man to score a hat-trick of tries in a game that England won 8–0. (Using modern rugby scores, the victory would 82–0.)

His record did not stand for long – his team-mate George Burton scored four tries in the same match – but Vassall had made a statement of intent. He was an England regular for two years, his final international appearance coming against the same opponents in Swansea in 1882.

He then spent a decade as RFU treasurer and wrote a chapter in Rev. Frank Marshall's *Football: The Rugby Union Game*, which was the first book dedicated to the sport and a key early tome.

ENGLAND STATISTICS

December 1882 – March 1887

England appearances: 12

England points: 4 (2 tries)

ALAN ROTHERHAM

Heralded for revolutionizing halfback play during the 19th century, Alan Rotherham was inducted into the World Rugby Hall of Fame in 2011 under the theme of creativity and innovation.

Throughout history there are individuals who make their mark in sport, and without doubt Rotherham (pictured centre, holding the ball) is one such person. More than a century before the game of rugby became professional, the Oxford graduate changed the face of the sport forever with his thoughts on how halfbacks should play.

It was during his time playing for Oxford University that Rotherham began to make waves within the rugby world. The Coventry man — in tandem with captain Harry Vassall — proposed a style of play that saw the halfbacks act as a link between the forwards and three-quarters. In such a way, the passing game of the backs could be utilized while the forwards would ensure that possession was won and maintained.

Today, such a concept and philosophy seems obvious and simple, but back in the 1880s when Rotherham was promoting the idea it was revolutionary. It led to the halfbacks becoming the pivots and playmakers of the team. The style became so well known, in fact, that it was dubbed "the Rotherham game".

Rotherham would play three seasons for Oxford as well as playing club rugby for Coventry and Richmond. International honours followed, with his debut for England taking place against Wales in 1882. Unsurprisingly, "the Rotherham game" was adopted by England and during his 12 matches for the national side the halfback claimed eight victories.

It was to be a short-lived international career, however. Towards the end of the 1880s England were in dispute with the International Rugby Board, and by the time they returned to the international arena in 1890 he was out of the side.

But the now-qualified barrister's legacy would live on. Many spoke of his brilliant halfback play, arguing that no finer performance had been given. In 2011, Rotherham received full recognition for his services to rugby when he was inducted into the IRB Hall of Fame. In keeping with his flowing style, he was added under the theme of creativity and innovation. A fitting tribute to a revolutionary rugby player.

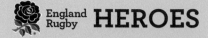
JAMES PETERS

The first black man to represent England, James Peters was a huge inspiration to those who followed him – particularly England's Vunipola brothers.

James Peters's standing in the game of rugby was brought home in late 2013. Stuart Lancaster, the England Head Coach, has made a virtue of the team's history and has encouraged a series of presentations about the most interesting and inspirational characters to have worn the shirt.

Peters's story struck a chord with the Vunipola brothers. As it was told, both Mako and Billy became visibly emotional, and the latter has spoken of the pride he takes in following in the footsteps of a man who made his England debut in 1907.

It is an astonishing story. After his father, a Jamaican lion-tamer, was mauled to death in a training cage, the youngster was sent to an orphanage in Southwark. Excelling at sport from an early age, Peters moved to Bristol and then Plymouth. He was a superb athlete, holding records in the mile race as well as the high and long jumps.

He was clearly good enough to play for his country, though the journey to international honours was not a smooth one. Peters was selected to play against South Africa in 1906, but this was withdrawn when the Springboks objected to playing against a black man.

A year later he did make his England debut, against Scotland. Again, the selection was far from universally popular and his second match, against France, was to be his last.

Yet it was a testament to his skill and perseverance that Peters continued to play rugby, even after losing three fingers in a dockyard accident in 1910.

Eventually, though, he grew tired of the politics of rugby union and moved back to his native north-west to play rugby league, turning out for Barrow and St Helens.

His was a career that did not hit the heights his talent deserved. Unfortunately for trailblazers, such is often the case – but few can doubt the fact that Peters has had a profound effect on members of the current squad.

ENGLAND STATISTICS
March 1906 – January 1908
England appearances: 5
England points: 6 (tries)

CYRIL LOWE

This First World War flyer was the England record holder for appearances and tries scored by the time he retired – and is thought to be the inspiration for Biggles.

Cyril Lowe was a quite astonishing individual. Standing at just 1.67m and weighing 54kg, he was an unlikely rugby union international but would write his name in history as one of the most attacking and creative wings ever to play the game.

An outstanding sportsman who won three Blues while at Cambridge, he made his England debut against South Africa in 1913. He was not an immediate success. Considered by many to be simply too small, he was jokingly referenced by fellow Dulwich College old boy P.G. Wodehouse, who wrote in a poem that the "shock of the afternoon came when somebody passed to Lowe".

But Lowe made light of that and burst into life during England's last three games before the outbreak of war, scoring eight tries against Ireland, Scotland and France. His tally of eight tries and back-to-back hat-tricks are both still Five/Six Nations records, held jointly with Scotland's Ian Smith.

That game against France, in Paris on 13 April 1914, would prove particularly poignant. Of the 30 men who started, 11 would not survive World War One and three would die before the year was out.

Lowe himself survived, embarking on a glittering career in the Royal Air Force. He is officially credited with shooting down nine German aircraft, although some reports claim 30 and Lowe himself believed the true tally was 21.

Wounded in action in March 1917, Lowe was awarded the Distinguished Flying Cross (DFC) and Military Cross (MC), the latter for "conspicuous gallantry and devotion to duty ... courage and self-sacrifice of a very high order". His bravery and character also reportedly inspired W.E. Johns to create one of the great fictional characters, Biggles.

Lowe returned to international rugby in 1920, and although six years had passed his pace was still electrifying. He scored nine tries in ten games, signing off from rugby with two more Grand Slams in 1921 and 1923.

Lowe retired with two England records, for appearances and tries. The latter stood until 1990, when it was beaten by Rory Underwood, another RAF man.

A hero for rugby and his country, Lowe is one of the finest men to wear the Red Rose. He died in 1983, aged 91.

ENGLAND STATISTICS
January 1913 – April 1923
England appearances: 25
England points: 58 (18 tries,
1 drop goal)
Grand Slam winner: 1913, 1914,
1921, 1923

ENGLAND STATISTICS
February 1914 – April 1914
England appearances: 2
England points: 0
Grand Slam winner: 1914

ARTHUR HARRISON

The only England rugby union international to be awarded the Victoria Cross, Harrison was killed during the raid on Zeebrugge in 1918.

After every international, Stuart Lancaster and his coaching team presents the Arthur Harrison Award to the team's finest defender. It is named in honour of the only English rugby union international to be awarded the Victoria Cross, and reflects Lancaster's stated ambition to connect the current side to its history and their predecessors in the shirt.

Few have done more for their country than Harrison (pictured bottom row, third from the left). A fine all-round player, he represented United Services, Rosslyn Park and Hampshire. A career naval officer, he was keen to indulge his passion for rugby at any given opportunity. While playing for Rosslyn Park, he gave his address as: HM Torpedo Boat No. 16, Portsmouth.

His international debut came on Valentine's Day 1914 against Ireland at Twickenham. King George V was at Twickenham for the first time since his coronation in 1910, and Prime Minster Herbert Asquith also attended the match.

Harrison performed well, particularly in the scrum, and in April he played against France. Eleven of the men who started the game would die in the Great War, among them Harrison.

Against France he impressed again, helping England to their second successive Grand Slam.

Four months later, on 28 August, he was involved in the Battle of Heligoland, where his ship, HMS *Lion*, helped sink the German boat *Cöln*.

A Lieutenant Commander, Harrison was mentioned in dispatches after the Battle of Jutland in 1916, but it was for his part in the raid on Zeebrugge, 22–23 April 1918, that he is remembered. Struck by a fragment of shell and presumed to be dead, Harrison stunned his men by recovering consciousness, taking command of his party and silencing the enemy guns. Harrison and all but two of his men were killed in the mission.

Harrison was posthumously awarded the Victoria Cross. The citation reads, "Already severely wounded and undoubtedly in great pain, Lt Cdr Harrison displayed indomitable resolution and courage of the highest order in pressing his attack, knowing as he did that any delay in silencing the guns might jeopardize the main object of the expedition."

It is fitting that almost a century on from his sacrifice, Harrison is remembered by his successors in the England jersey.

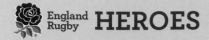
WAVELL WAKEFIELD

Wavell Wakefield revolutionized back-row forward play during an inspirational career as England captain, leading his country to back-to-back Grand Slams.

Wavell Wakefield's standing in the game is best demonstrated by the fact that he was the first Englishman inducted into the International Rugby Hall of Fame, in 1990.

He had played his last game of Test rugby some 63 years previously, but his legacy was clear. To start with, he revolutionized how a back row should play. This was previously considered a static position, but Wakefield used his athleticism to become a powerful force in the loose. He developed defensive systems for the forwards, particularly when it came to using a fast open-side flanker to put pressure on the opposition fly-half from the set piece.

Aged just 16 when the First World War broke out, Wakefield was a captain in the RAF and joined Harlequins – a club for whom he would go on to play 136 times, 82 of them as captain.

His England debut followed in 1920, and he subsequently made 31 appearances for his country – at that time a record. Cyril Lowe had previously held the record with 25 appearances, and he sent Wakefield a congratulatory telegram for beating his record in 1926, with a match against Wales.

Captain of the Cambridge team during the 1922–1923 season, "Wakers" was a key part of the England side's astonishingly successful spell in the 1920s. He lost just two of his first 20 Test matches, playing for a team that claimed the Grand Slam in 1921, 1923 and 1924.

Wakefield was captain for the latter two of those triumphs, and he led his side on 13 occasions – a record that stood until the 1980s, when it was surpassed by Bill Beaumont.

Wakefield helped to set up the Middlesex Sevens tournament in 1926 and was a hugely talented all-round sportsman, playing cricket for the Marylebone Cricket Club, becoming President of the Ski Club of Great Britain, and being the RAF 440 yards dash champion.

On his retirement from sport, he was Conservative MP for Swindon between 1935 and 1945, and after that for St Marylebone. Knighted in 1944, he was appointed Baron Wakefield of Kendal on his retirement from parliament in 1963.

President of the RFU during 1950 and 1951 and President of Harlequins between 1950 and 1980, he also served on the IRB Board for a number of years. An extraordinary career.

ENGLAND STATISTICS
January 1920 – April 1927
England appearances: 31
England points: 18 (6 tries)
Grand Slam winner: 1921, 1923, 1924

Wavell Wakefield shows the attacking skills that helped
England to back-to-back Grand Slams. Rugby historian
Barry Bowker described him as "A complete footballer...
with all the attributes – strength, weight and speed – of a
great forward. He was a master of the art of dribbling with
pace, was up with his backs to share in an attack and took
and gave passes well."

ENGLAND STATISTICS

January 1934 – March 1937
England appearances: 10
England points: 0

TUPPY OWEN-SMITH

Captain of the England rugby team and a Test cricketer for South Africa, the full-back goes down as one of the greatest sportsmen of the inter-war years.

A doctor, South African Test cricketer and captain of the England rugby union team, Tuppy Owen-Smith had an eventful life.

Born in South Africa, Owen-Smith studied at Diocesan College in Rondebosch and then attended the University of Cape Town. His athletic prowess was apparent from an early age. He excelled at both cricket and rugby, representing his university at both sports. International honours would follow later.

In 1929 Owen-Smith came to England and his first sporting endeavours were as a cricketer rather than a rugby player. He played five Tests for South Africa during the summer tour, finishing with a batting average of 42. Such was his level of performance that Wisden named him Cricketer of the Year for 1930.

Later that same year Owen-Smith returned to England once more, this time as a Rhodes Scholar, studying medicine at Oxford University. Unsurprisingly he earned his Oxford Blue in both cricket and rugby, but the talented sportsman also turned his hand elsewhere: he added athletics and boxing awards to the trophy cabinet.

Owen-Smith finished his studies at St Mary's Hospital Medical School. By now, the newly qualified doctor was turning heads on the rugby pitch. England were showing an interest and in 1933 the full-back made his debut for England.

An attack-minded player, Owen-Smith would go on to make 10 appearances for England, earning praise for his dynamic runs and aggressive play. In 1937 the doctor was given the honour of captaining England, completing his remarkable transition from South African cricketer to skipper of the England rugby team. Eight years prior, he had arrived on England's shores as a Test series opponent, and now he was leading their rugby team on to the field.

Owen-Smith would captain England three times, his final match taking place at Murrayfield against Scotland. He bowed out a winner, leading England to a 6–3 victory.

ENGLAND STATISTICS
February 1949 – April 1954
England appearances: 23
England points: 3 (1 try)

JOHN KENDALL-CARPENTER

A highly successful forward and England captain, John Kendall-Carpenter played a role in making the dream of a Rugby World Cup a reality.

Not many men can captain their country and not have it be the highlight of their rugby career. But John Kendall-Carpenter (pictured middle row, fourth from the left) left a very distinct legacy in the sport, his involvement continuing long after his final international in 1954.

After retirement, he worked as an administrator, serving as President of the RFU between 1980 and 1981.

His toughest professional challenge, however, came when he was Chairman of the committee that organized the first Rugby World Cup. His was the responsibility for delivering the tournament in New Zealand both on time and on budget.

He did so, and was asked to do the same for the 1991 tournament. This he did with great success until his untimely death in May 1990, by which time the groundwork had been laid.

His playing career had also been enormously successful and he won three successive Blues playing for Oxford between 1948 and 1950. The *Guardian*'s David Frost recalled his tackle on J.V. Smith in the second of those matches, a game Oxford won 3–0.

"Smith slipped his man, side-stepped two coverers and seemed certain to cross at the corner and bring at least an equalizing try. Cambridge hats were already in the air and Oxford's supporters were dumb with horror but then at the last possible moment Kendall-Carpenter dived and took man and ball into touch a yard from the line."

An England debut arrived at Lansdowne Road that same year, and he played at No. 8, although his next five Tests would all be at prop. From the Calcutta Cup match in 1950, Kendall-Carpenter played only in the back row, rather than at the centre of the scrum.

He captained his country and his only international try arrived against Scotland at Murrayfield in 1952.

That would have been enough of an achievement for most people, but Kendall-Carpenter went on to make an enduring mark off the field. He was posthumously inducted into the IRB Hall of Fame.

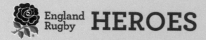

DICKIE JEEPS

A Lions legend who made the England No. 9 shirt his own, scrum-half Dickie Jeeps was a superb ball-player respected the world over.

Dickie Jeeps wasn't even really meant to play in South Africa in 1955. Unable to force his way on to the England team, he was selected very much as the third-choice scrum-half for the Lions' tour of South Africa. He was there to play only if others needed a rest or were injured.

That was the theory, anyway. By the time Jeeps retired from international rugby seven years later, no one had made more Test appearances for the Lions than his 13.

The key in 1955 was his understanding with Cliff Morgan, the great Welsh fly-half. The man who would go on to become the voice of the Barbarians was a superb, creative player and the fulcrum of the Lions side. He immediately struck up a superb understanding with Jeeps, establishing them as very much the first-choice halfback pairing.

From the moment Morgan led the crowds in a half-hour singsong on arrival at Johannesburg airport, they were a Lions side that captured hearts and minds like few others.

The four-Test series was drawn 2–2, but it was a thrilling affair,

the Lions scoring a remarkable 26 tries. Jeeps returned home with his reputation bolstered, and made his England debut the following year against Morgan's Wales.

England lost that day and Jeeps spent a year on the sidelines as a result, but he would not taste defeat again on the international stage for some time. The team twice beat Australia, and it was July 1959 before the Lions lost three Tests to New Zealand. The All Blacks nicknamed him "India rubber man", due to his elusive running. High praise indeed!

In the meantime he was a key part of England's Grand Slam-winning side of 1957, with victories in Cardiff and Dublin followed by victories over France and Scotland at Twickenham.

Jeeps was appointed England captain in early 1960 and led the team for two years. During that time, the team won five, drew four and lost four of the 13 games played.

A talented schoolboy batsman, Jeeps finished his international career with the Lions, starting all four Tests on the tour of South Africa in 1962. In later life, he was President of the RFU, serving between 1976 and 1977.

ENGLAND STATISTICS
January 1956 – March 1962
England appearances: 24
England points: 0
Grand Slam winner: 1957
Lions tours: 1955, 1959,
1962

ENGLAND STATISTICS

January 1956 – March 1963

England appearances:	20
England points:	18 (6 tries)
Grand Slam winner:	1957
Lions tours:	1959

PETER JACKSON

An unorthodox but brilliant runner, Peter Jackson won acclaim with both England and the Lions, but his crowning glory was a stunning, match-winning try against Australia in 1958.

To give you an idea of quite how light Peter Jackson was on his feet, all you need to know is that he was nicknamed "Nijinsky" during his playing days – not after the horse, but rather the Russian ballet dancer.

The wing was a simply sensational runner with ball in hand, elusive, quick and unpredictable. Described by one journalist as "the zaniest runner of all time", he was a vital part of the England team that claimed some memorable scalps in the late 1950s.

Few of them were more memorable than the victory over Australia at Twickenham in 1958. England were hanging on grimly for victory despite having just 14 men as they paid for some brutal Australian tackling. Facing scrum after scrum under their own posts, they needed to release the pressure – and Jackson did so in inimitable style.

His run from his own line to the opposition's was so good he had the opportunity to beat Australian full-back Rod Phelps not once but twice. No wonder footage of the day shows the crowd throwing their caps in the air in celebration!

Moving to Coventry in 1954, he made his international debut two years later, against Wales. A try followed in his second Test, versus Ireland, but it was in the 1957 Five Nations that he really hit the heights: his three tries helped England claim their first Grand Slam since the 1920s.

In 1959 he embellished his reputation still further with a fine display during the Lions' tour of New Zealand. In just 16 matches he scored 14 tries, including two in three Tests against the All Blacks.

Dropped in 1960, Jackson reclaimed his place for the Calcutta Cup match in 1961, before returning to feature in four games during the 1963 Five Nations and playing a key role in a length-of-the-field score against Wales.

A draw in Dublin meant England could not claim a Grand Slam, but they won the title and Jackson went out on a high. After such a fine player career, he worked as secretary and president of Coventry.

ENGLAND STATISTICS
February 1961 – April 1969
England appearances: 34
England points: 9 (3 tries)
Lions tours: 1962

BUDGE ROGERS

The first English rugby player to be honoured by the Queen, Budge Rogers OBE played a record 34 times for his country and captained them on seven occasions.

Budge Rogers's success in the shirts of England, the Barbarians and Bedford can be tracked back to the noticeboard at Bedford School.

There his schoolteacher would pin a bar chart showing the amount of tackles made by each player. Rogers and a school friend were always neck and neck for tackles made, which was not bad considering he was a scrum-half at the time.

So, when the school needed a flanker for one particular game, they looked at the chart and realized Rogers might be worth a shot. He never looked back, going on to play on the flank his entire career for Bedford and England.

His debut for England came in just his second season in the Bedford first team. He even scored in the defeat to Ireland, finishing smartly after a kick was charged down. From that point on, he was a fixture in the side throughout the 1960s.

His approach was fully committed, and he has explained why he was so successful. "I don't think there was a game I didn't enjoy. I was very committed. Rugby was all that mattered. Jobs went on but weren't

given the priority they could have been. I trained very hard. My game was all about being fitter than the others, tackling and not doing much else. I always trained Christmas afternoon, as we had a trial first week in January."

England's most successful season was 1963, when the Five Nations title was won. Yet the Grand Slam was not achieved, a 0–0 draw in Dublin ensuring England fell just short of the ultimate glory.

Appointed captain for the first time in January 1966, Rogers would go on to lead his country on seven occasions, winning two of them.

Rogers was also a Lion in 1962, playing two games against South Africa while he was a great servant to the Barbarians, making 25 appearances for the club between 1961 and 1971.

His ability and character were recognized when he was appointed an OBE in 1969, the first English rugby union player to receive such an honour from the Queen.

After retirement Rogers remained in rugby, going on to be Chairman of Selectors, England team manager and President of the RFU.

ENGLAND STATISTICS
February 1969 – February 1976
England appearances: 36
England points: 36 (10 tries)
Lions tours: 1971

DAVID DUCKHAM

Combining grace with power and with a sidestep to die for, David Duckham shone for England and the British & Irish Lions between 1969 and 1976.

It says all you need to know about the skill and wonder of David Duckham that after he starred for the Barbarians against New Zealand in 1973, the Cardiff crowd christened him "Dai". The knowledgeable support agreed he was worthy of the ultimate respect of being called "one of us".

Indeed, footage of that game proves what an extraordinary talent Duckham was. The camera actually loses him mid-run as he produced a step so sleek the cameraman bought it from 100 yards away.

These were displays that the Twickenham crowd had long come to expect. Duckham, who played for Coventry throughout his career, scored on his England debut against Ireland in 1969 and soon established a wonderful centre partnership with John Spencer.

It was a relatively conservative era for the English side, which meant that Duckham's creativity and guile were even more welcome and acknowledged.

He scored two tries in his first Calcutta Cup match against Scotland in March 1969, and few were surprised when he was picked for the Lions' tour of New Zealand two years later. He started three matches on the wing in that victorious series, scoring 11 tries in 16 games in total. His haul of six against West Coast-Buller remains a Lions record, which he shares with J.J. Williams.

One of his most memorable days came when he scored two tries in the win over France in February 1973. It was a result that put England on course for their historic five-way tie for the Five Nations that year, when every team won their two home games and lost their two away ones.

His last try for England came in the famous win over Australia in January 1976, with his last appearance for his country coming the following month at Murrayfield.

Made an MBE after retirement, he became Honorary President of the rugby charity Wooden Spoon, which improves the lives of disadvantaged children and young people in the UK and Ireland.

David Duckham steps past New Zealand fly-half Ian Stevens as he demonstrates his legendary running ability at Twickenham in 1973. Duckham scored 10 tries for England and an astonishing 11 for the Lions on the 1971 tour of New Zealand.

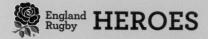

BRIAN STEVENS

One of the most fearsome scrummagers in the game, Brian Stevens is a Cornish Pirates and England legend who memorably scored the decisive try in that famous win in Auckland in 1973.

Props aren't meant to charge over the line to secure Test victories on New Zealand soil, and not many of them started their professional careers on the wing.

With all due respect to wonderful English props down the years, from Jason Leonard to Dan Cole, they seem rather more at home in the thick of things than the wide open spaces – but Brian "Stack" Stevens never did conform to expectations.

He didn't last long on the wing at Cornish Pirates, but the lessons he learnt there clearly stayed with him as he moved to the front row.

The highlight of his international career came in Auckland in 1973, some four years after he had made his England debut. It was a try of rare skill as England profited from a poor defensive kick, Stevens exchanging passes with second row Christopher Ralston before cutting through the home defence to score and put the seal on a 16–10 victory.

There were plenty of other highs, though. His debut came against South Africa in 1969, and he captained the side against Griqualand West on tour in the same country two years later, scoring a try to mark the occasion.

The final game of that tour was against South Africa at Ellis Park. Though England had won their six previous games, few now gave the team a chance, but in front of a capacity crowd of 77,400 the players triumphed 18–9. In seven matches over a 24-day period, England had scored 166 points, conceded just 58 and won every single one of their games. It was a stunning success.

Stevens was also a Lion and a Barbarian. He toured New Zealand with the Lions in 1971, although he had to turn down the chance to do so to South Africa three years later.

Stevens was a hugely likeable character who famously tells the story of how he used to hitch lifts to England training in Coventry in lorries carrying cauliflowers. His England career continued until 1975, and on retirement he had accumulated 25 appearances and two tries. That made him the most-capped Cornishman of all time, the wing's loss being the front row's gain.

ENGLAND STATISTICS
Dec 1969 – March 1975
England appearances: 25
England points: 8 (2 tries)
Lions tours: 1971

ENGLAND STATISTICS

January 1971 – March 1980

England appearances:	43
England points:	19 (5 tries)
Grand Slam winner:	1980
Lions tours :	1974, 1977

TONY NEARY

Tony Neary was a stalwart for England and the Lions throughout the 1970s, and his total of 43 appearances for his country was a record when he retired after winning the Grand Slam in 1980.

England flanker Tony Neary's international career ended in the most spectacular manner imaginable.

When England headed to Paris for the final game of the 1980 Five Nations, they were well aware that it was 16 long years since they had last won in the French capital.

The 1970s had mostly been a decade of frustration, but having beaten Ireland in their opening game the team knew that victory in Paris would open the door to a potential Grand Slam.

England were focused, and recovered from an early try by French skipper Jean-Pierre Rives after just three minutes to lead 14–7 at half-time. Key to this was an astounding effort by the English scrum – who were down to just seven men, Roger Uttley receiving stitches for a head wound. The French were kept at bay under their own posts, which allowed Nigel Horton to slot a drop goal that would prove decisive.

Neary was key to that stunning forward effort, with England going on to scrape past Wales before defeating Scotland at Murrayfield to seal a Grand Slam. It was to be Neary's last act in an England shirt – but what a way to sign off!

His international career had begun almost a decade earlier, when he played against Wales in Cardiff in 1971. A busy, bustling nuisance of a flanker, Neary went on to captain his country in seven internationals during 1975 and 1976.

He also toured twice with the Lions, in 1974 and 1977, while he led the pack that faced the Barbarians in their first ever home game at Twickenham, to mark the Queen's Silver Jubilee in 1977.

Neary also went on to be a member of the famous "North" team that defeated the touring All Blacks in 1979 at Otley, while he played his club rugby for Broughton Park. The flanker also went on to represent Lancashire, but he will be remembered for his achievements with England – and, above all, for being part of that Grand Slam-winning side in 1980.

A true England legend.

ENGLAND STATISTICS

March 1971 – January 1981

England appearances:	31
England points:	4 (1 try)
Grand Slam winner:	1980
Lions tours:	1974, 1977, 1980

FRAN COTTON

A tall and powerful prop who went on three Lions tours, Fran Cotton was ahead of his time in terms of physical conditioning – while he is also the subject in perhaps the most famous rugby photograph of all time.

The name Fran Cotton brings one specific image to mind. It is of the England prop preparing for a lineout while playing for the Lions against New Zealand Juniors in 1977. In it you can barely see Cotton; rather a strange figure caked head to toe in mud, two eyes peeking out through the matted hair.

It instantly became an iconic shot, while it also summed up Cotton's commitment to the cause.

The son of a rugby league player, Cotton recognized early on that superior physical conditioning could set him apart from his competitors. While a student of Loughborough College, the prop used their equipment to give him a vital edge – and it was one that England certainly appreciated.

The Lions did, too. Cotton made his debut in the Calcutta Cup in March 1971, and his performances in the victories over Australia and New Zealand two years later ensured he would be heading to South Africa with the Lions in 1974.

He became an integral part of that wonderful side as they won 21 of their 22 matches, playing in all four Tests.

Indeed, his versatility can be demonstrated by his Lions career. In South Africa he packed down at tighthead in all four Tests, before playing three at loosehead in New Zealand three years later. He was also skilled enough with ball in hand to represent the England Sevens side in 1973.

Yet despite Cotton's undoubted skill and prowess, he seemed destined to end his international career without silverware to show for it. That all changed in 1980, when he started every game as England charged to the Grand Slam under the leadership of Bill Beaumont.

This was to prove somewhat of a last hurrah for Cotton. Viral pericarditis – originally misdiagnosed as a heart attack – forced him out of the Lions tour in 1980 and a hamstring injury brought his England career to a close against Wales the following year.

He went on to form rugby leisure company Cotton Traders alongside former team-mate Steve Smith with great success, and was Lions team manager on their victorious tour to South Africa in 1997.

ENGLAND STATISTICS
January 1972 – February 1976
England appearances: 24
England points: 8 (2 tries)
Lions tours: 1974

ANDY RIPLEY

Rugby's first rock 'n' roll superstar, charismatic No. 8 Andy Ripley was one of the most entertaining characters to play for England.

Andy Ripley was a larger-than-life character whose physical prowess was such that he tried out for the Boat Race aged 50, and the outpouring of grief when he finally succumbed to prostate cancer aged just 62 said it all.

The stories about Ripley are nearly as memorable as the man himself. There are several from the stunning 1974 Lions tour of South Africa, in which the invitational side were unbeaten in 22 matches and won the Test series 3–0. One day, the touring party went into a local township and all had returned by nightfall – except for Ripley. "When he eventually turned up, he was wearing nothing but a leopard skin," said hooker Bobby Windsor. "He'd given away every last bit of his Lions kit – tracksuit, shirt, shorts, socks, trainers – the lot. What a fantastic bloke."

On the same tour, Ripley turned up to an official function looking as if he had just come from the beach. Tour manager Alun Thomas warned him, "You will wear the tour blazer, grey trousers and tie to the next function – or else." Ripley did as he was told, and wore only those three items, turning him into a legendary figure among team-mates and with supporters.

He was also an astonishing all-round sportsman. Going to a football-playing school, he only picked up a rugby ball when he was 19, but his progress was rapid. He made his England debut six years later against Wales at Twickenham, while he also represented the victorious English side in the inaugural Rugby World Cup Sevens at Murrayfield the following year, running the length of the field for one astonishing score.

The scorer of two tries for England, he played in the two stunning victories in Johannesburg and Auckland in 1972 and 1973.

After retirement he competed on BBC's *Superstars* several times, competing in the 400m hurdles, triathlon, canoeing, sailing, water-skiing, tennis and basketball. He commentated on rugby for French television. And he was elected President of Rosslyn Park, the club where he spent his entire playing career, arriving for the annual dinner on his Triumph motorbike and wearing jeans and a t-shirt.

A wonderful character and player.

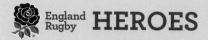

MIKE BURTON

An uncompromising prop for Gloucester, England, the British & Irish Lions and the Barbarians, Mike Burton earned a reputation as a devastating scrummager during a stellar career.

There are few greater legends down in Gloucester than Mike Burton. They know a fair bit about prop forwards at Kingsholm, and it is instructive that Burton is still talked about in reverential tones in the West Country.

Such reverence is hardly surprising. He made 360 appearances for the club, topping that tally up with 40 for Gloucestershire, with whom he won the John Player Cup on two occasions. He was also a key member of the English squad in the early 1970s and the Lions in their victorious tour of South Africa in 1974.

Yet as Burton well knows, he will also be remembered in part for being the first Englishman to be sent off in an international. That moment of history came in Sydney against Australia in 1975. The game had begun with a brawl between the two sets of forwards and after just three minutes Burton was dismissed for a late tackle on Australian winger Doug Osborne. The disciplinary hearing that followed ruled no further punishment was necessary.

Burton's England debut had come three years earlier against Wales, and that summer he was a member of the undefeated touring side of South Africa. England beat the Springboks 18–9 at Ellis Park in what was one of the highlights of Burton's career.

In 1974 he toured South Africa again with Willie John McBride's Lions, a series in which the tourists went 22 games unbeaten.

He continued to excel for England, gaining revenge over Australia with victory at Twickenham in January 1976 as the Wallabies were beaten 23–6 in a hugely impressive display.

Burton did not feature for England in 1977, but he returned to play two more games the following year, against France in Paris and Wales at Twickenham. The latter was to be his 17th and final England appearance.

Since retiring, Burton has become a successful businessman in the fields of corporate hospitality, sports travel and entertainment, specializing in rugby.

ENGLAND STATISTICS
January 1972 – February 1978
England appearances: 17
England points: 0
Lions tours: 1974

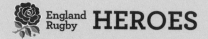

BILL BEAUMONT

Beaumont was an inspirational captain who led England to the Grand Slam in 1980 and went on to be a formidable Lions skipper, as well as a member of the IRB board and RFU Chairman.

When writing a summary of Bill Beaumont's career, it is hard to know where to start. You could, of course, talk about his days at Fylde in Lancashire, where he first came to prominence, or when he captained the North of England to victory over the All Blacks in 1979.

Or you could focus on the fact he was the first Englishman in 50 years to be appointed captain of the Lions when he was chosen to lead the tour to South Africa in 1980.

Then there are the roles after rugby, serving as England's representative on the IRB Council before becoming RFU Chairman.

The other option is to mention his television work, and his role as a captain on *A Question of Sport* for 14 years. At the same time, he ran his family's textiles business and served as honorary President of the Wooden Spoon charity.

But eventually, the focus must come back to 1980, and England's first Grand Slam since 1957.

Beaumont had made his international debut five years previously, as a 22-year-old against Ireland. He played in three Tests on the Lions' tour of New Zealand in 1977 and was appointed England captain a year later, succeeding Roger Uttley.

A leader both in word and deed, Beaumont has gone down in history as one of the finest captains England has ever had in any sport. Yet third- and fourth-place finishes in the Five Nations meant few were prepared for what would follow in 1980.

Under Beaumont's leadership, England shocked the world. Ireland and Wales were defeated at home, France and Scotland away in quite glorious style. It was England's first clean sweep in 23 years. "Billy led by example," remembers team-mate Paul Dodge. "He would be the first over the top and was always at the bottom of rucks and mauls."

It was inevitable Beaumont would be appointed Lions captain for the 1980 tour of South Africa, and he played in 10 of the 18 games.

Injury brought his career to a premature end, but he has since gone on to become a respected administrator and is currently the RFU President after serving on the IRB, Six Nations and Rugby World Cup boards with distinction.

Awarded both an OBE and a CBE, he is truly one of English rugby's finest and most recognizable figures.

ENGLAND STATISTICS
January 1973 – January 1982
England appearances: 34
England points: 0
Captain of Grand
Slam-winning side: 1980
Lions tours: 1977, 1980
Lions captain: 1980

Bill Beaumont in full flight was a tough man to stop. "Billy was a great guy – a real top man. That whole England team was a bunch of characters, everyone was a character and he held it together... the perfect captain." John Scott, England No. 8 in 1980.

ENGLAND STATISTICS

February 1973 – March 1980

England appearances:	23
England points:	8 (two tries)
Grand Slam winner:	1980
Lions tours:	1974

ROGER UTTLEY

England forward and sometime captain, Lions tourist, charity fundraiser, Lions and England assistant coach and national team manager – Roger Uttley has done it all.

Roger Uttley's skill as a rugby player was perhaps best demonstrated on the 1974 Lions tour to South Africa. An imposing 1.92m tall, Uttley had built a fine career as a rampaging second row. He was selected for that tour in his normal position and played there in two warm-up games. Then came the type of lightbulb moment that can change perceptions and the course of a series, as Uttley was switched to blindside flanker, a position new to him.

It was to prove a superb decision and he stayed there for all four Tests, scoring a try in the final game of what was an unbeaten tour. That cemented his status as a Lions legend, but his place in English rugby history was already well on the way to being secured.

He first started playing rugby at 15 and his development was rapid after moving to the north-east to study at Newcastle College. Uttley played for Gosforth and, after a series of knockbacks, was picked to make his England debut against Ireland in February 1973. He remembers it well:

"One night, John Elders [the coach] came back from a selection meeting and said he was just dropping in to tell me I was playing in Dublin in 10 days! I walked back and Christine [his wife] said, 'You've gone white, but it's fantastic news.' But there was a slight feeling that I needed to put my money where my mouth was, as I had been asking for a call-up for so long, and that was rather daunting!"

He certainly did put his money where his mouth was, and was swiftly one of the first names on the team sheet.

Uttley was also chosen to captain his country on five occasions and continued his international career until 1980. It ended in the most glorious fashion imaginable with a first Grand Slam since 1957, achieved through gritty, gripping victories in Paris and Edinburgh.

Assistant to Jack Rowell when England reached the 1991 Rugby World Cup Final, he was also team manager during the 1990s. And he has also contributed to the sport with his numerous charity escapades, particularly those in memory of his former team-mate Andy Ripley. A true legend.

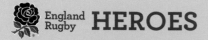
STEVE SMITH

Grand Slam winner, England captain and one of the most gifted scrum-halves of his generation, Smith was a hugely talented player who was picked for two Lions tours.

Like a number of players in his generation, Steve Smith will always look back on 1980 as a stunning high point of his career. England had gone 23 long years without winning a Grand Slam and had not gone particularly close to ending that sequence during the 1970s. But as a new decade dawned, so did new hope.

England began with victory over Ireland at Twickenham, scrum-half Smith establishing himself in the side with a fine try. Then came tight victories over France and Wales before the crunch match: Scotland in Edinburgh.

It was an incredibly close game, but in the end England emerged victorious 30–19, Smith scoring once again. It was a moment of triumph and hope, as England proved they could live with the best the world has to offer.

"We hadn't been close for so long, so for me personally, it was the best day of my rugby career," Smith said. "For the England supporters who had suffered so long, being in Edinburgh that night was fantastic."

It was also the culmination of Smith's journey to the top of his sport. The Sale player made his debut in 1973 – in the same game where Roger Uttley made his international bow, against Ireland in Dublin – but he played only nine games for his country until the end of 1979. However, he then went on to play in 19 consecutive games for England, his stunning performances in 1980 earning him a late call-up as a replacement for the Lions tour to South Africa.

He replaced Bill Beaumont as captain in 1982 and led the side on five occasions, winning games against France and Wales. His international career came to an end in March 1983, but his association with rugby was far from over as he set up Cotton Traders alongside former team-mate Fran Cotton.

At one point they supplied kit to over half the world's international sides, while Smith also became a television co-commentator. That was another field in which he enjoyed great success, and he was commentating when England won the 2003 Rugby World Cup.

ENGLAND STATISTICS
February 1973 – March 1983
England appearances: 28
England points: 8 (2 tries)
Grand Slam winner: 1980
Lions tours: 1980, 1983

ENGLAND STATISTICS

May 1975 – March 1979

England appearances: 14
England points: 48
          (3 conversions,
          14 penalties)

ALASTAIR HIGNELL

An astonishingly talented sportsman who made 14 appearances for England at full-back in the 1970s, Hignell became a highly successful commentator and charity fundraiser.

It was fitting that Alastair Hignell bade his farewell to rugby union on the same day as another true legend of the English game.

The cameras had spent much of 31 July 2008 focused on Lawrence Dallaglio as he brought the curtain down on his playing career in magnificent style, leading Wasps to victory over Leicester in the Premiership Final at Twickenham.

But they lingered on Hignell, too. As the Radio 5 Live commentator handed over to colleague Ian Robertson for the final time, the big screens at Twickenham split between him and Dallaglio, putting the two men together to rapturous applause.

It was Hignell's last commentary engagement, as he retired at the age of just 52 due to the onset of multiple sclerosis. He had fought the disease bravely for a decade, earning the respect of all in the game. He was awarded a CBE for services to rugby and charity, as well as the Professional Rugby Players' Association's Blythe Spirit Award for his "remarkable courage" in battling MS, and the Helen Rollason Award from the BBC.

It was a measure of his standing in the game that Dallaglio dedicated victory to Hignell that day.

"It is fitting that we should win and dedicate the victory to him," said Dallaglio. "He is a very special man."

Hignell's England debut had come more than 30 years previously, against Australia in Brisbane in 1975, in what became known as "The Battle of Ballymore".

He later described what happened: "The first lineout ball went straight over the top, and they all turned round and thumped each other. Then Mike Burton got hold of this guy and gave him the 'Kingsholm kiss'. It was mayhem. Bill Beaumont went off for stitches. And I still hadn't touched the ball."

Hignell went on to make 13 more appearances for England but was also a prodigiously talented cricketer, playing for Gloucestershire throughout his rugby career. Three times he scored more than 1,000 runs in a summer, once making a century against the great West Indies team of the 1970s.

A natural in the commentary box, he enjoyed a highly distinguished career with the BBC over a 23-year period until bidding the game farewell alongside Dallaglio.

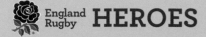
PETER WINTERBOTTOM

One of the finest flankers of his generation, Winterbottom became the second man to reach 50 appearances for England and starred on two Lions tours to New Zealand.

With his shock of blonde hair and all-action style, Peter Winterbottom cut a familiar figure on the international scene in the 11 years after his debut for England in 1982.

He had a seemingly inexhaustible appetite for work and the energy to match, and his status in the game is best illustrated by the regard in which he was held by both New Zealand and South Africa, two countries in which he played club rugby during his illustrious career.

His value to England or the Lions was never in any doubt, however. Indeed, the Yorkshireman was afforded a rare honour when he was asked to lead the Lions out for the third Test in New Zealand in 1993, to mark his final professional match. By that point, he made 58 appearances for England, becoming the second man behind Rory Underwood to reach the half-century mark.

His debut came against the Wallabies in 1982, starring for the Lions on their tour of New Zealand a year later and playing in 12 of their 18 games.

A regular during the 1987 Rugby World Cup, scoring twice against the USA, Winterbottom came into his own as England began to enjoy a resurgence under Geoff Cooke late in that decade.

Forming a formidable back-row partnership alongside Mickey Skinner and Dean Richards, he revelled in being a key man of an experienced team that peaked in 1991.

That was the year England won the Grand Slam under the captaincy of Will Carling, and he played in every game as Cardiff and Dublin were sacked, with France and Scotland beaten at home.

That ensured England were well set for the Rugby World Cup on home soil, and as excitement grew to fever pitch they came so close to winning it. In the end, though, Australia outdid them in the Final, but Winterbottom could console himself with a fine individual tournament in which he started every game bar the Pool Stage battle with Australia.

He signed off after another Lions tour of New Zealand and his record number of games at openside stood until Neil Back beat it in 2003.

ENGLAND STATISTICS
January 1982 – July 1993
England appearances: 58
England points: 13 (3 tries)
Grand Slam winner: 1991, 1992
Lions tours: 1983, 1993

ENGLAND STATISTICS
February 1984 – March 1996
England appearances: 85
England points: 210 (49 tries)
Grand Slam winner: 1991, 1992,
                          1995
Lions tours: 1989, 1993

RORY UNDERWOOD

The RAF Flight-Lieutenant was the first man to play 50 times for England, while his searing pace helped him score a record 49 tries for his country.

Rory Underwood lived for speed. His day job was in the RAF, but he was best known for playing on the wing for England for an entire generation.

Between 1984 and 1996, no one in the English game could touch Underwood. His achievements are legendary: he was for some time the most capped Englishman and the scorer of the most tries, and he and his brother Tony were the first siblings to play for the Red Rose since 1937.

An exhilarating, electrifying runner, he was part of an England side that won Grand Slams in 1991, 1992 and 1995.

He made his international bow in 1984 against Ireland, his first try coming in his second match against France at the Parc des Princes. But Underwood struggled to score regularly in his early international career because England relied on a forward-based game that did not give their back three much opportunity to run with the ball.

That all changed after the 1987 Rugby World Cup, in which Underwood scored twice against Japan but was unable to prevent a quarter-final defeat to Wales.

Geoff Cooke and Will Carling helped to transform English rugby and Underwood was an undoubted beneficiary, scoring nine tries in as many games during 1988. In 1989 he grabbed the headlines with a stunning five-try haul against Fiji, matching the world record.

A star for the Lions the following year, he scored five tries for England in 1990, including two spectacular efforts against Wales. Then, having just fallen short in their pursuit of a Grand Slam, England finally got there in 1991.

That same year Underwood helped them reach the Rugby World Cup Final, winning his 50th cap against Scotland in a bitterly tense semi-final victory, although they couldn't quite get over the line against Australia in the Final.

A Lion again in 1993, he appeared in all three Tests and scored a vital try against the All Blacks in the second.

In 1995 England continued their northern hemisphere domination, winning another Grand Slam and claiming a stunning victory over South Africa in Pretoria. Yet the team then came up short in this, Underwood's third Rugby World Cup, Jonah Lomu proving too good in the semi-final.

Nevertheless, Underwood can be content with his astonishing record. He is a genuine superstar.

Leaving defenders in his wake, Rory Underwood makes another dash for the line. His dazzling pace helped him to score a record 49 international tries.

ENGLAND STATISTICS
November 1984 – May 1989
England appearances: 14
England points: 0
Lions tours: 1989

GARETH CHILCOTT

A hugely popular prop for Bath, England and the Lions, Gareth Chilcott improved as his career progressed and was a key member of his country's Rugby World Cup 1987 squad.

A huge character who upheld rugby's finest traditions, Gareth Chilcott was one of the most popular players for England during the 1980s.

He left school aged 15 and worked as a lumberjack and nightclub doorman while working his way through the ranks at Bristol, before internal strife at his hometown club led him to leave for Bath alongside Nigel Redman and Richard Hill.

It was to be the making of the man and one of the key catalysts for Bath's stunning success; he played 374 times for the club. His fellow players included Stuart Barnes, Jeremy Guscott, Andy Robinson and Jon Hall, and Bath went on to become the dominant force of the decade. England attempted to cash in on their success.

Chilcott, Redman and Hill all made their international debuts in 1984, the former two in a 19–3 defeat to Australia at Twickenham.

Chilcott was unable to establish himself in the team immediately, and had to wait some 16 months before receiving a second cap, in the Five Nations against Ireland. This was to prove a far happier occasion, England winning 25–20 at Twickenham.

Chilcott now became a regular squad member, and there was little doubt he would be included in the England squad for the 1987 Rugby World Cup despite being one of the players briefly left out of the side following an overly physical match in Cardiff, which led to heavy criticism.

He was a starter against Japan and USA, but then Wales did for England – and Chilcott – in the quarter-finals, winning 16–3 in Brisbane.

There then followed another period where Chilcott was in and out of the side, although he showed his best in victories over France and Ireland during the 1989 Five Nations. Again, though, Wales proved a step too far as they dashed England's Grand Slam dreams.

Always a popular member of any squad, Chilcott had a personality that seemed tailor-made for a Lions tour – and so it proved when he was chosen for the 1989 tour of Australia. He made five appearances on tour as a crucial member of "Donal's donuts" midweek side, scoring his only international try against New South Wales Country in his final game.

On retirement Chilcott became a successful after-dinner speaker and businessman.

ENGLAND STATISTICS
January 1985 – March 1993
England appearances: 55
England points: 12 (3 tries)
Grand Slam winner: 1991, 1992
Lions tours: 1989, 1993

WADE DOOLEY

Standing 2.02m tall, "The Blackpool Tower" was a key part of the England side that recorded Grand Slam victories in the 1991 and 1992 Five Nations.

It doesn't take a genius to work out that a man who was nicknamed "The Blackpool Tower" was a rather imposing physical specimen. A police officer with the Lancashire Constabulary in Blackpool, the second row was given the nickname due to his giant frame and domineering presence in the lineout.

During his youth, Dooley had mostly played rugby league, largely due to the fact he grew up in the north-west – a hotbed for the sport. But at the age of 19, he made the transition to rugby union, spending the majority of his career at Preston Grasshoppers under the watchful eye of former England international Dick Greenwood.

It was in 1985 that Dooley made his international bow, taking to the field against Romania at Twickenham. Deployed in the second row, he went on to form a formidable partnership with fellow police officer Paul Ackford. Stopping criminals and opposition forwards are rather different hazards, but the two players proved equally effective at both.

Dooley's performances were not going unnoticed, and it came as no surprise when he was called up for the 1989 Lions tour of Australia. The second row played in the final two Tests against the Wallabies, helping the Lions secure a famous series win.

More success was to follow, but this time in the white of England. In 1991 Dooley helped the Red Rose soar to a Grand Slam triumph in the Five Nations, their first since 1980. One year later, and the same outcome occurred, the second row once again playing a pivotal role.

The Lions came calling once again in 1993, but Dooley was forced to head home early to attend his father's funeral. The second row's absence was undeniably a huge loss to the touring party, but his replacement proved to be a worthy substitute. Like Dooley, that man would go on to become another of England's great second rows: Martin Johnson. Dooley could bring the curtain down on his international career knowing that England's future was in safe hands.

ENGLAND STATISTICS
January 1985 – March 1997
England appearances: 71
England points: 396 (2 tries,
33 conversions,
86 penalties,
21 drop goals)
Grand Slam winner: 1991, 1992,
1995
Lions tours: 1989, 1993

ROB ANDREW

Rob Andrew is an England and Lions legend who won three Grand Slams and whose metronomic kicking proved vital to England's success in the early 1990s.

Rob Andrew's England achievements seemed likely to remain untouched for ever. Amassing a total of 396 Test points, steering his country through three Rugby World Cups and with 86 penalties to his name, he even had the honour of kicking what was then considered the most celebrated drop goal in English rugby history, in the 1995 quarter-final against Australia.

Still, if his record had to be beaten, there was some satisfaction in knowing that the man responsible was his protegé, Jonny Wilkinson.

Among the many legacies of Andrew's time as Newcastle player and Director of Rugby was Wilkinson. A mentor to the young fly-half, Andrew watched with pride as this precocious talent developed into a Rugby World Cup-winning talisman.

Andrew had played that same role in the England team for more than a decade. Some had initially considered him to be too small for the role, but his metronomic boot and tactical mind kept him in the team and England on the front foot. His tackling was brutal too.

Andrew made his England debut against Romania in 1985, marking it with four penalties and two drop goals, and went on to start every game of the next two Five Nations.

The fly-half really came into his own when Will Carling was appointed captain, and he was called up as a replacement for the 1989 Lions tour helping to vanquish Australia.

Two years later, he and Carling were hoisted aloft by joyful supporters as the team finally claimed the Grand Slam.

England were set fair for Rugby World Cup glory, but despite his drop goal sealing victory in the semi-final over Scotland, Australia were to prove too strong in the end.

Two more Grand Slams followed and then Andrew wrote his name in the record books with a 27-point haul against South Africa in 1994.

Then came another Rugby World Cup, and another glorious drop goal – this time against the Wallabies in the final seconds of the quarter-final. Unfortunately, New Zealand and Jonah Lomu then proved a step too far.

Andrew played one more game after that Rugby World Cup, against Wales in 1997. He ended his career with a full trophy cabinet and all manner of individual honours.

Andrew has continued to make a significant contribution to rugby, firstly in the role of RFU Elite Rugby Director and then as RFU Professional Rugby Director.

ENGLAND STATISTICS
April 1987 – June 1995
England appearances: 64
England points: 4 (1 try)
Grand Slam winner: 1991,
 1992, 1995
Lions tours: 1989, 1993

BRIAN MOORE

The hooker forged a reputation as being one of the hardest men in the game during his 64 appearances for England, earning the nickname "Pitbull".

If we look back through the history of English rugby, there are surely few players who can compete with the physicality and toughness of Brian Moore. Over an eight-year period, the hooker became a regular for England.

His ferocity may have won him the moniker "Pitbull", but Moore is a rather more complex and intriguing character than his nickname would suggest. Unlikely though it may seem, he used to read Shakespeare to his team-mates before matches.

When it was game-time, though, Moore lived up to his name. England first came calling in 1987, as they prepared to take on Scotland. In front of a packed Twickenham, Moore started his career in the white jersey with a 21–12 victory over the Scots.

Despite a quarter-final exit in the 1987 Rugby World Cup, success and victory would follow Moore throughout his career. Two years after his England debut, he was called up to the British & Irish Lions. The hooker toured with them in 1989 for the trip Down Under, helping the side to claim a historic series win against Australia.

Famously, during preparations for a lineout in the second Test, an Australian spectator threw a full can of beer at him, which just missed his head. Brian's reaction was to pick the can up, turn to the crowd, open the beer, toast the crowd, drink the beer and throw the empty can back. Says team-mate Jeff Probyn, "For that and many other reasons, Brian would always be my No. 1 hooker."

Returning a victorious Lion, Moore's success flowed into England as they won back-to-back Five Nations Grand Slams in 1991 and 1992. By now, Moore had formed a formidable front row alongside Jason Leonard and Jeff Probyn. Together the trio made a truly destructive force, and with their help England reached the 1991 Rugby World Cup Final.

However, an expectant Twickenham was left disappointed as Australia pipped England to glory in what was one of the few defeats in Moore's career. Despite the loss, 1991 had been a brilliant year for Moore and his efforts were recognized when he was crowned Rugby World Player of the Year. After a triumph in 1992, a third and final Grand Slam came in 1995.

Moore bade farewell to international rugby after the 1995 Rugby World Cup, but by the end the statistics said it all: a World Cup Finalist, a victorious Lion and a three-time Grand Slam champion.

ENGLAND STATISTICS
January 1988 – March 1992
England appearances: 21
England points: 12 (3 tries)
Grand Slam winner: 1992

MICKEY SKINNER

The flanker was renowned for being one of the game's toughest tacklers, and he played a vital role in England's run to the 1991 Rugby World Cup Final and their back-to-back Grand Slams.

His nickname of "Mick the Munch" means that it doesn't take long to comprehend what type of player Mickey Skinner was. The flanker was capable of rocking players to the core and making their bones shudder – so much so that his hit on France's Marc Cécillon was dubbed simply "The Tackle".

It was a vital moment in the 1991 Rugby World Cup quarter-final, a game where the levels of tension were desperately high. "It was truly confrontational, brutal and ferocious – probably the most physical game I've ever been involved in," said hooker Brian Moore in later years. The two teams had to contain themselves from physical confrontation in the tunnel, but on the pitch there was no holding back.

The crucial moment came with the scores locked at 10–10 and France camped in England's 22. After a series of scrums, French No. 8 Cécillon picked up from the base and darted round to the right. There he was met by Skinner, who had been brought in to replace Dean Richards due to the quality of his tackling. The flanker hit Cécillon perfectly, driving him back well over five metres to the roars of 20,000 travelling English supporters.

"The tackle broke their hold on the game," said Skinner of a hit that could be heard down the Champs-Elysées. "We had two or three scrums in our own 22 and we were under the cosh."

England, who went on to beat Scotland in the semi-finals, could not follow that with victory over Australia in the Final, but Skinner had made his point.

His international career began four years earlier when he was taken to the Rugby World Cup as a last-minute replacement, though he never made it on to the pitch. A year later he made his international debut against France in Paris during the Five Nations as England went down to a narrow 10–9 defeat. They would finish the tournament in third place, still hunting for their first Five Nations triumph since 1980.

In 1991 that thirst for a Grand Slam was finally realized as England conquered all on their route to the Final.

The Rugby World Cup cemented Skinner's reputation, his popularity among the public rising throughout the tournament.

He brought the curtain down on his international career with a second Grand Slam in 1992, scoring a try in the decider against Wales. But he will always be remembered for that one stunning tackle.

ENGLAND STATISTICS
January 1988 – March 1997
England appearances: 72
England points: 54 (12 tries)
Grand Slam winner: 1991, 1992,
1995
Lions tours: 1993

WILL CARLING

England's youngest captain led his country to three Grand Slam titles and formed a devastating centre partnership with Jeremy Guscott during a stellar career.

Most 22-year-olds would be content simply to be a member of the England team, looking to establish their place in the squad or firm up a role in the side. Not Will Carling.

Instead, he relished being given the honour of captaining England against Australia in just his eighth Test. It went rather well. So well, in fact – England scoring four tries on their way to a 28–19 victory – that Carling was to captain them another 58 times. It's a record that no one, not even the great Martin Johnson, has come close to beating.

Just how successful was Carling?

He won 75 per cent of his matches as skipper. Hugely charismatic, he understood the value of strong leadership. "I was just lucky to have experienced, strong characters in the side who managed to ensure our success," Carling has said since, but that underplays his contribution.

Certainly until his arrival England were not among the great over-achievers in world rugby. Yet Carling and Geoff Cooke changed all that. A fleet-footed centre, Carling also formed a superb partnership with Jeremy Guscott. They played together 43 times for England, Carling joking that he did the tackling for both of them while the "Prince of Centres" took the glory.

Yet there was plenty of glory for Carling in the Five Nations. Grand Slam champions in 1991, 1992 and 1995, England exerted a vicelike grip on the competition during the early part of the decade.

The first victory was particularly satisfying, the culmination of a process that had begun with a win against Australia during Carling's first game as captain.

There was criticism from some quarters for the style of play, but England equalled the tournament record of 12 tries in 1990 and bettered that tally by three in 1992. The one disappointment was that England did not win the Rugby World Cup, despite making the Final under Carling's guidance, on home soil in 1991.

One of England's finest leaders and a captain who dragged the game into the professional era, Carling refused to be fazed by anything.

Will Carling issues a rallying cry to his team-mates during his hugely successful spell as captain. When Carling stepped down as England captain, the RFU President Bill Bishop said, "He was an inspirational choice as captain by Geoff Cooke in 1988 and his record speaks for itself."

ENGLAND STATISTICS
June 1988 – November 1995
England appearances: 8
England points: 4 (1 try)
Rugby World Cup-winning
assistant coach: 2003
Grand Slam-winning
assistant coach: 2003
Lions tours: 1989
Lions tours as
assistant coach: 2001, 2005

ANDY ROBINSON

The flanker enjoyed success with England and the Lions but made his mark in 2003 as right-hand man to Sir Clive Woodward, and became Head Coach in 2004.

Nowadays Andy Robinson is more likely to be remembered for his time as a coach, but the flanker enjoyed his own fair share of success as a player, appearing eight times for England in the late 1980s and early 1990s.

Prior to gracing the international stage, Robinson played his rugby for Loughborough Students. From there he moved on to Bath in 1986, where he would spend the entirety of his club career. At the West Country side, Robinson enjoyed great success, captaining the club to Courage League and Pilkington Cup triumphs.

Captaincy and leadership suited Robinson well: he had also led Loughborough Students during his time with the university. Unsurprisingly his performances did not go unnoticed and in 1988 England came calling.

The flanker would make his debut against Australia in Sydney, but it proved to be a day to forget as the Red Rose suffered a 28–8 defeat at the hands of the Wallabies.

Robinson, though, was forging a strong reputation. Despite being only 1.74m, the flanker was more than making up for his size with some impressive displays. A year after his England debut, Robinson was voted European Player of the Year. The flanker was also called up for the 1989 Lions tour to Australia.

The trip Down Under saw Robinson make six appearances for the Lions, but none in the three Tests. Further England appearances followed, but it was as a coach where Robinson would cement his place in the record books, playing a vital role as assistant to Sir Clive Woodward when England claimed the William Webb Ellis trophy in 2003. As forwards coach he had responsibility for the pack – who simply bullied everyone in front of them during the tournament.

Robinson would go on to coach England on 22 occasions between 2004 and 2006 after Woodward's exit, and subsequently enjoy further spells in charge of Scotland and Bristol. He was also a fine member of the Lions coaching staff in 2001 and 2005, cementing his reputation as one of the sharpest minds in rugby.

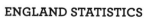

ENGLAND STATISTICS

May 1989 – October 1999

England appearances: 65

England points: 143 (30 tries, 2 drop goals)

Grand Slam: 1991, 1992, 1995

Lions tours: 1989, 1993, 1997

JEREMY GUSCOTT

"The Prince of Centres" was a wonderfully graceful, direct player who could find gaps in the tightest of defences and inspired both England and the Lions to memorable victories.

There is no greater compliment for a young English centre than to be mentioned in the same breath as Jeremy Guscott.

"It's great to be compared to someone of such calibre," said Jonathan Joseph, the latest to be given the moniker "the new Guscott" after his sterling exploits early in 2015. Certainly Joseph would love to emulate some of Guscott's achievements.

The holder of 65 caps for England and eight for the Lions, Guscott scored 31 international tries as well as three drop goals – one of which, for the Lions in South Africa, was rather special indeed. He was the winner of three Grand Slams and a part of three Rugby World Cup squads, and what made his exploits all the more remarkable was that he did it all without seeming to break sweat.

Possessing remarkable balance, footwork and agility, Guscott was able to run round covering defenders rather than through them, creating space for himself and his team-mates to exploit.

The impression was that international rugby came easily to Guscott. He thrived from the very beginning, scoring a hat-trick on his debut against Romania in 1988. He certainly wasn't fazed when, with just a solitary cap to his name, he was called out to join the Lions a year later, starting the final two Tests in that historic series victory over Australia.

He had eight tries to his name after his first eight Tests, and silverware was to follow. Grand Slams were won in 1991, 1992 and 1995 as England became unquestionably the finest side in the northern hemisphere.

The only disappointment during that period was the 1991 Rugby World Cup Final, won by Australia despite England's attempts to play vibrant, attacking rugby.

A Lions tourist again in 1993, Guscott played his part in a second Rugby World Cup in 1995 as England reached the last four before running into Jonah Lomu.

On a personal level, though, Guscott's best moment was yet to come. His drop goal to win the second Test – and seal a series victory – against South Africa in 1997 was an historic moment in rugby history. It was, said Rob Andrew, "a defining moment in sport".

Guscott bowed out after his third Rugby World Cup, but it was typical that his final game saw him throw an outrageous dummy and streak in from 95 metres. Truly, a prince among men.

Jason Leonard breaks through the Uruguayan defence during the 2003 Rugby World Cup. Highly respected by his England team-mates, Jonny Wilkinson says of the Fun Bus: "I don't think he'll mind me calling him a hero. But he is certainly one of the great heroes of the English game."

ENGLAND STATISTICS
January 1992 – October 1999
England appearances: 44
England points: 25 (5 tries)
Grand Slam winner: 1992, 1995
Lions tours: 1997

TIM RODBER

A powerful forward who conquered the world with the England Sevens team in 1993, Tim Rodber then went on to take the 15-a-side game by storm with England and the Lions.

A modest character who once claimed he was simply "an army officer who is able to play international sport", Tim Rodber was a hugely talented rugby player who excelled throughout the 1990s.

It was in 1992 that he made his England debut in a 25–7 victory at Murrayfield. A back row who later in his career shone at lock, Rodber had an athleticism that shone through and it was this dynamism that led him to be head-hunted for the England Sevens team.

It proved to be a shrewd move: in 1993 England claimed the Rugby World Cup with a team that also featured the likes of Lawrence Dallaglio and Matt Dawson.

Two years later and – after playing a huge part in England's victory in Pretoria in 1994 – Rodber was again gunning for Rugby World Cup glory, but this time in the 15-man game. He played in six games during England's run to the semi-finals, but the might of Jonah Lomu and New Zealand proved too much in the semi-final.

Rodber found himself back in South Africa in 1997, this time as a member of the Lions squad hunting for a series victory against the world champions. Now thriving as a No. 8, Rodber had established himself as captain of the midweek side, but the Test spot seemed to be in the hands of Wales forward Scott Quinnell.

Yet Rodber produced a series of inspired performances, while Quinnell was forced to leave the tour through injury. He seized his chance, playing in the first two Tests – both of which were won – in an all-English back row alongside Dallaglio and Richard Hill.

After the event, Rodber looked back on the tour – and particularly captaining the midweek side – as one of his greatest experiences. "Sitting around the changing room and realizing that these great names from British and Irish rugby were looking to me for a lead [made me] very proud. There was a great spirit on that tour."

Two years on and Rodber again came up against South Africa, this time in the 1999 Rugby World Cup quarter-finals. It proved a stage too far for England, and was Rodber's last international appearance, although he was able to lift the Heineken Cup with Northampton the following year.

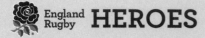

MARTIN JOHNSON

The captain's captain, Martin Johnson is the only England skipper to lead his side to Rugby World Cup glory, doing so in Sydney in 2003. A world-class lock, he inspired those around him and intimidated the opposition. They don't come any better.

You don't win the Rugby World Cup without a superb captain, and in Martin Johnson England were fortunate to have one of the finest skippers of the modern game. The Leicester lock had never taken a step back in his career and his leadership during the 2003 Rugby World Cup was simply inspirational.

That final against Australia in Sydney was the last of his 92 games, and the culmination of an international career that had begun against France a decade earlier. Indeed, his debut sums up his character well. He was supposed to be playing in a B international on the Friday night, but a late injury to Wade Dooley led to him being called up for the senior side. He had time for a 20-minute lineout session with his team-mates and was momentarily concussed after an early clash of heads, but he was still the finest player on the pitch.

A key member of the England sides that won Grand Slams in 1995 and 2003, he will always be associated with Sir Clive Woodward and Jonny Wilkinson. Said Wilkinson after Johnson announced his international retirement: "The guys would have done anything he asked. We followed his lead. His ability to stand up to intimidation and to intimidate himself was incredible. For our side it was respect and a great belief he was on your side. There were guys who could lift more, who could run quicker, but no one could stand on the field and have the effect he did."

His physicality and set-piece strength were his main attributes as a player, but Johnson is the only man to captain two Lions tours, and it was what he brought with his personality that was key.

With England down to six forwards after two sin bins and time running out against New Zealand in June 2003, Woodward's side had to withstand a series of scrums five metres out as they looked to protect their two-point lead. Johnson's instruction to his men? "Just push." Asked later what was going through his head, he replied, "My spine."

He was appointed England Head Coach in 2008 and led the team to the quarter-finals of the 2011 Rugby World Cup, but it is as a player and inspirational Rugby World Cup-winning captain he will be remembered.

ENGLAND STATISTICS

January 1993 – November 2003

England appearances:	84
England points:	10 (2 tries)
Rugby World Cup winner:	2003
Grand Slam winner:	1995, 2003
Lions tours:	1993, 1997, 2001

England's record appearances holder, Jason Leonard, says of the 2003 Rugby World Cup-winning captain: "Martin is the most inspirational England player of his time. He was a world-class player and a world-class captain."

ENGLAND STATISTICS
November 1993 – November 2003
England appearances: 51
England points: 15 (3 tries)
Rugby World Cup
winner: 2003
Grand Slam winner: 1995, 2003
Lions tours: 1997

KYRAN BRACKEN

A Rugby World Cup winner in 2003, the scrum-half claimed over a half a century of appearances and captained England on three occasions.

To say there was a lot of competition for the England scrum-half shirt in the late 1990s and early 2000s would be a gross understatement. In Kyran Bracken, Matt Dawson and Austin Healey, England had three of the finest No. 9s in world rugby. Indeed, all three were involved in the Lions' 1997 tour of South Africa when Bracken was called up as an injury replacement for Rob Howley.

Considering the competition, Bracken's achievement in obtaining over 50 caps for England is therefore even more impressive than it first seems.

His talents were always obvious. Aged just 13, he was offered a rugby scholarship to Stonyhurst College in Lancashire. This prestigious rugby school has produced no fewer than 16 international players, and Bracken was joined there by fellow future Rugby World Cup winners Will Greenwood and Iain Balshaw.

By 1993 Bracken was turning heads with his performances for Bristol and he made his international bow against New Zealand. An ankle injury forced him off, however, and it took the scrum-half three months to return to full fitness.

Yet he was a squad regular from that point on, embracing professionalism by giving up his job as a solicitor to move to Saracens in 1996. He was unfortunate to miss out on selection for the Lions tour in 2001 and was instead given the honour of captaining England during the tour of North America.

In the build-up to the 2003 Rugby World Cup, the fight for the No. 9 jersey intensified as England swept all before them. Dawson may have been selected for two Lions squads, but Bracken was impressing for Sir Clive Woodward's side after recovering from a career-threatening injury. Most notably, the live wire was supreme in England's victories over Australia and New Zealand during the summer tour.

For the Rugby World Cup Down Under, Dawson did keep his starting berth. But Bracken's presence undoubtedly spurred the scrum-half on to greater heights. And Bracken was entrusted with leading the side through their vital Pool game against South Africa, making a crucial tackle early on that saved a try and gave England a huge advantage.

A calming influence, he had a wealth of experience at the highest level, and the fact that England could call upon a player like Bracken from the bench demonstrated just how strong a squad Sir Clive had.

ENGLAND STATISTICS
February 1994 – November 2003
England appearances: 66
England points: 83 (16 tries,
1 drop goal)
Rugby World Cup
winner: 2003
Grand Slam winner: 2003
Lions tours: 1997, 2001,
2005

NEIL BACK

A ferocious tackler and unbeatable at the breakdown, 2003 Rugby World Cup winner Neil Back was one of the greatest back-row players ever to represent England.

When Neil Back made his international debut in 1994 against Scotland, eyebrows were raised as the 1.77m flanker made his way on to the pitch. Many argued he was too small, not big enough to make it at the highest level, and Back would make just four international appearances over the next two years.

But those who knew him were well aware the flanker would not walk away from a challenge.

By 1997, he was back with a bang. A member of the victorious Lions squad in South Africa, Back flew home from the southern hemisphere knowing the doubters had been silenced.

His form provided England with a formidable back row. Lawrence Dallaglio and Richard Hill completed the trio and the "Holy Trinity" was formed. Back was the perfect complement to Dallaglio and Hill, providing the two powerhouses with a speedy ally who could steal the ball at the breakdown.

With Back in the side, England won back-to-back Six Nations titles in 2000 and 2001. But it was in 2003 that the flanker and his country enjoyed their greatest year. It began with a Six Nations Grand Slam as eyes turned expectantly towards the Rugby World Cup in Australia. Going into the tournament, England had defeated all the southern hemisphere sides. The nation expected glory.

Back and his team-mates did not disappoint, living up to their billing as pre-tournament favourites and returning with the William Webb Ellis trophy.

Back himself was in supreme form, playing in six of England's games and scoring two tries as the Holy Trinity were reunited for the semi-final and Final once Hill had recovered from a hamstring injury. His fitness was such that he played all 100 minutes of the Final against Australia as Jonny Wilkinson's drop goal sealed victory.

A year later, Back announced his retirement from the international stage, but by 2005 he had been tempted to return for the Lions tour of New Zealand. At 36, he became the oldest ever Lion as he turned out for Sir Clive's side. A fitting swansong for one of the game's greatest flankers.

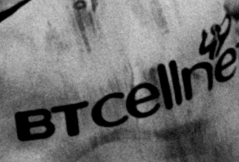

ENGLAND STATISTICS
March 1994 – October 2007
England appearances: 75
England points: 142 (7 tries,
                       16 conversions,
                       22 penalties,
                       3 drop goals)

Rugby World Cup
winner: 2003
Grand Slam winner: 1995, 2003
Lions tours: 1997, 2001

MIKE CATT

The man who kicked the ball dead to seal victory in the 2003 Rugby World Cup Final, Mike Catt's versatility won him 75 caps during a 13-year England career.

It is a testament to Mike Catt's talent that he turned out for England in no fewer than four positions and thrived in all of them. Be it at fly-half, centre, wing or full-back, Catt made his mark on the international stage.

It was in 1994 against Wales that Catt made his first appearance for England. Born in South Africa, he qualified for England due to the fact his mother was English. South Africa's loss was England's gain.

His debut came as a replacement fly-half, but a year later he shone at full-back as England romped to the Five Nations Grand Slam. Lions honours followed in 1997 and 2001, with his versatility making him an asset few could rival.

By the time 2003 came around, Catt was the experienced head England required and showed his class as he helped Sir Clive Woodward's side claim the trophy.

When a cool head was required, Woodward turned to Catt. That was never clearer than in the quarter-final against Wales, where Catt ran the game after being called upon for the second half. That secured him a starting spot at inside centre for the

semi-final with France, while he also came on as a replacement in the Final against Australia.

Catt even had the honour of kicking the ball dead in the last act of the Final to spark those wild scenes of celebration we all remember so clearly.

As the 2007 Rugby World Cup drew nearer, sceptics were beginning to write Catt off, claiming that at 36 he would be unable to have the same impact. He proved them all wrong, being voted the Premiership's Player of the Season for the 2005/2006 campaign and helping to lead England to another Final.

As he took to the field against South Africa, he became the oldest player ever to compete in a Rugby World Cup Final. England would succumb to defeat, and Catt announced his retirement from the international arena.

His influence endures. He has since extended his career with England, becoming a coach under Stuart Lancaster – and he can still be seen on the Twickenham turf during a match, ferrying instructions to the players from the bench. The likes of Jonathan Joseph and Anthony Watson cannot fail to learn from him.

ENGLAND STATISTICS
November 1995 – October 2007
England appearances: 85
England points: 85 (17 tries)
Rugby World Cup
winner: 2003
Grand Slam winner: 2003
Lions tours: 1997, 2001,
2005

LAWRENCE DALLAGLIO

The only man to play every minute of England's victorious 2003 Rugby World Cup campaign, Lawrence Dallaglio was perhaps the perfect back-row player.

If you could build a prototype back row, you would probably come up with someone who looks very much like Lawrence Dallaglio. Standing 1.92m tall and weighing about 114kg, he had a physicality that was astonishing. Then there was his character. A natural leader who wore his heart on his sleeve, Dallaglio would often be spotted with a tear in his eye during the national anthems, and he brought that same emotional intensity to bear on the opposition.

His England career lasted some 14 years, if we include his international bow made for the Sevens side during their victorious Rugby World Cup campaign in 1993. At that stage a raw but lavishly gifted young talent, Dallaglio made his debut for the 15-man team in 1995.

Two years later and Dallaglio became a Lion, playing in all three Tests on the victorious tour of South Africa.

Appointed national team captain by Sir Clive Woodward in 1997, he was forced to give up the honour due to off-field issues two years later.

Martin Johnson succeeded him, and Dallaglio was able to focus entirely on his rugby. Cemented as first-choice No. 8 by the 1999 Rugby World Cup, he came into his own in 2003.

His status in the squad was such that he was the only man to play every minute of England's games, including the 111–13 victory over Uruguay in the Pool Stages. Part of the "Holy Trinity" back row, alongside Neil Back and Richard Hill, Dallaglio was simply sensational during the tournament. "We felt like it was our destiny to win it," he said after the event, and he had done as much as anyone to make that a reality.

He was far more than just a powerful, physical player: it was his superb break and inside pass which led directly to Jason Robinson's score in the Final. Team-mate Matt Dawson and he are the only two players to win Rugby World Cups at both Sevens and senior level.

Dallaglio returned from international retirement to be a part of the 2007 side that stunned rugby by reaching the Rugby World Cup Final against the odds. He finally retired from all rugby a year later, having led Wasps to the Guinness Premiership title in his final game. It was a fitting way for one of the all-time greats to sign off.

"His leadership was his personality and his performance on the pitch. He was a big influence on the whole squad." Lawrence Dallaglio receives high praise from his England team-mate and captain Martin Johnson.

ENGLAND STATISTICS
March 1995 – June 2006
England appearances: 54
England points: 0
Grand Slam winner: 1995, 2003
Lions tours: 1997, 2005

GRAHAM ROWNTREE

A tough and reliable prop who made more than 50 appearances for England, Graham Rowntree is now the coach tasked with getting the England pack in shape for the Rugby World Cup on home soil.

Graham Rowntree's achievements as a player are in serious danger of being eclipsed by his prowess as a coach.

Not content with 54 appearances for England and another three for the Lions during an 11-year international career, he is now a vital member of Stuart Lancaster's coaching team.

Under his watch, the England pack have gone from strength to strength and now believe that they can beat the very best in the world on their day.

Rowntree has been central to that, overseeing everything during his intense but highly effective sessions.

His coaching ability was recognized when Sir Ian McGeechan appointed him set-piece coach for the 2009 Lions tour. Four years later, Warren Gatland asked him to be forwards coach.

His career has come full circle since making his debut in 1995 as a replacement for the great Jason Leonard against Scotland at Twickenham. He proved something of a lucky charm in those days, winning 11 of the first 12 Tests he was involved in, including the two Rugby World Cup Pool matches he started in 1995.

Called up for the Lions in 1997, Rowntree was a regular in the midweek side but failed to win a Test cap in South Africa.

His rivalry with Leonard drove both players to new heights, and it is a mark of his ability that Rowntree was able to claim a half-century of appearances despite being up against a man often called the finest prop ever to play the game.

Rowntree made three appearances in the 1999 Rugby World Cup, but he then lost his place in the squad for two years. After recovering, he forced his way back into the team in 2001. And in the build-up to the 2003 Rugby World Cup he put in a particularly memorable performance in the victory in Wellington, where England stayed strong at the scrum despite being reduced to eight forwards.

But he still missed the cut for the 2003 Rugby World Cup squad, a decision Sir Clive Woodward has described as the hardest he had ever had to make.

Not one to go out on a low, Rowntree fought back and played in all three Lions tests in 2005 before retiring in 2007. Then it was coaching, in an England career that may soon stretch over 20 years.

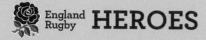

MARK REGAN

Mark "Ronnie" Regan was a "boisterous" hooker who came out of international retirement to star in England's run to the 2007 Rugby World Cup Final.

For a member of the England front row, there is no finer feeling than marching forwards as the opposition scrum crumples under the pressure.

With that in mind, it is hardly surprising that Mark Regan remembers the 2007 Rugby World Cup fondly, and the quarter-final with Australia in particular.

Famously aggressive and vocal, Regan knew that England – particularly with Andrew Sheridan in inspired form – could dominate the Wallabies at the set piece. And he was right.

"It was a wonderful feeling, being part of an England pack who had the Aussie lot on toast," he later recalled of a game dominated by the England scrum en route to a 12–10 victory. "I remember Lote Tuqiri, that bloody big wing of theirs, saying to little Josh Lewsey: 'Why don't they give you the ball, so I can smash seven bells out of you?' And Josh, bless him, pointed to the scrum and replied: 'Why would anyone want to give me the ball over here when that's happening over there?' Great stuff."

Regan wasn't even really meant to be there. A Lion in 1997, he had retired from England duty in 2004 after being a member of the squad that had won the Rugby World Cup a year previously, only to return when Brian Ashton was appointed Head Coach.

He did so because of the possibility of a repeat of 2003, something very few people outside the team believed could happen. And it very nearly did: France were defeated in the semi-finals before South Africa proved a step too far in the final. Yet it was a wonderful last hurrah for Regan, who always gave the impression he appreciated what rugby had given him.

"I'm still buzzing from it," he told the *Independent*. "A World Cup Final, at this stage of my career? Who'd have thought it? And leading out the Baa-Baas at Twickenham, with all my family in the stand and my kids as mascots, and beating the Springboks into the bargain?"

It was a glorious farewell for one of English rugby's most entertaining characters – and the Australians remember it all too well.

ENGLAND STATISTICS
November 1995 – February 2008
England appearances: 46
England points: 15 (3 tries)
Rugby World Cup
winner: 2003
Grand Slam winner: 2003
Lions tours: 1997

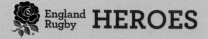

MATT DAWSON

England's most capped scrum-half played a vital role in the 2003 Rugby World Cup win and scored a stunning try in the Lions' series victory in South Africa.

The ability to execute tough skills under intense pressure separates the good from the great, and in the final minutes of the 2003 Rugby World Cup Final, Matt Dawson proved he could deliver just when it mattered most.

The move that would lead to Jonny Wilkinson's drop goal was a set piece that had been rehearsed a thousand times before, but it still needed someone to make a decisive break. That man was Dawson.

The lineout had been claimed, the ball driven up the middle. But England were still too far out for Wilkinson to kick for glory with any certainty. That was when Dawson came into his own, making a darting break that gained an extra 15 metres. The ball was taken forward again by Martin Johnson, and this time Dawson was in position at the base of the ruck. His pass to Wilkinson was perfect and the rest, as they say, is history.

It was the crowning glory in a fabulously successful career.

A Sevens Rugby World Cup winner in 1993 alongside Lawrence Dallaglio, he made his Test debut in 1995 and played in every game as England won the Five Nations the following year.

Originally selected as backup for the Lions tour of South Africa in 1997, Dawson forced his way into the starting line-up for all three Tests – and in the first of those he produced perhaps the cheekiest score in rugby history. His overhead dummy was outrageous, but it fooled four South African defenders and cleared the way for Dawson to score in the corner to seal a famous victory. In the second Test it was Dawson who passed the ball to Jeremy Guscott for the series-sealing drop goal, and he scored again in the final Test.

It was a truly stunning series on an individual level, and he continued in the same vein with the England team. His rivalry with Kyran Bracken drove both players on to new heights. Dawson's standing within the side was such that he captained his country in the 2000 Six Nations in the absence of the injured Johnson.

Three years later, Dawson and England were ready for glory – and they took their chance brilliantly.

ENGLAND STATISTICS
December 1995 – March 2006
England appearances: 77
England points: 101 (16 tries, 6 conversions, 3 penalties)
Rugby World Cup winner: 2003
Grand Slam winner: 2003
Lions tours: 1997, 2001, 2005

ENGLAND STATISTICS
November 1996 – February 2008
England appearances: 35
England points: 37 (6 tries,
                         2 conversions,
                         1 drop goal)
Rugby World Cup
winner: 2003
Grand Slam winner: 2003

ANDY GOMARSALL

A fine scrum-half whose best form in an England shirt came in the 2007 Rugby World Cup, where he played a key role in taking England to the Final.

Andy Gomarsall is almost certainly the only man in rugby history to go from playing for a pub team to a Rugby World Cup Final in just a few months.

Back in 2006, Gomarsall thought the curtain had been well and truly brought down on his England career. Just three years previously, he had been a Rugby World Cup winner, but a contract dispute with Worcester meant he was turning out for the White Hart Marauders to keep in shape.

Then an opportunity arose with Harlequins, and the scrum-half took it. His form soared, and he forced his way back into the international fold. By 2007 he was in the squad, albeit purely as backup.

But England struggled early on, and Brian Ashton turned to the then 33-year-old for the must-win Pool games against Samoa and Tonga.

With Jonny Wilkinson also returning to the side, England suddenly had a bright and effective halfback pairing, and it proved decisive. True, the forward effort was vital in the knockout stages as Australia and France were beaten, but Gomarsall and Wilkinson probed, directed and took charge with the scrum-half providing the kick that allowed Josh Lewsey to score against the French.

So while the days of amateurism had long gone, Gomarsall could still boast about going from a pub team to the Rugby World Cup Final. Truly Roy of the Rovers stuff!

Some 12 years previously, he had watched from the sidelines as England defeated Australia in the 1995 Rugby World Cup quarter-final. Uncapped at the time, he was summoned to South Africa in case Dewi Morris failed to recover from injury.

Morris did recover, but Gomarsall was emboldened, scoring twice against Italy on his international debut the following year. Two long spells in the international wilderness would follow, but Gomarsall was included in the squad for 2003, playing two games as England returned from Australia as champions of the world.

He thought his final international game had come in November 2004, but he was very much mistaken – and how England and the White Hart are grateful he was.

ENGLAND STATISTICS
November 1996 – October 2011
England appearances: 71
England points: 10 (2 tries)
Rugby World Cup
winner: 2003
Grand Slam winner: 2003
Lions tours: 1997, 2005,
2009

SIMON SHAW

A winner of more than 70 caps and a member of three Rugby World Cup and three Lions squads during a 15-year international career, Simon Shaw was one of the most respected locks in the game.

Considering everything he packed into a 23-year rugby career, it is astonishing to realize that Simon Shaw did not start to play the game until the age of 16.

He spent most of his youth in Kenya and Spain, but was spotted – which, given that he stands 2.02m tall, wasn't too hard – as a potential future rugby star when he moved to Godalming College in Surrey.

His economics teacher happened to have a brother who was a second row for Otago in New Zealand, and it wasn't long before Shaw found himself on the other side of the world starting out on his professional career.

"I barely knew rugby was amateur," Shaw has later said of that period. "I was driven to make a career out of it, even though there wasn't a career to be made. It was a bit naïve, but obviously it panned out."

It certainly did. Before long, he was playing for Bristol and missed out on selection for the 1995 Rugby World Cup only because of a knee injury. He moved to Wasps, where he would stay for 15 years, and then ended his club career with Toulon in France.

He made his international debut in 1996 and toured with the Lions the following year but struggled to hold down a regular spot in the England side over the next few seasons.

Not selected for the 1999 Rugby World Cup, he was called up to the 2003 squad only as an injury replacement for Danny Grewcock. In the tournament, he failed to play a single minute.

Named the Premiership Player of the Year in 2003/04, he forced his way into the Lions touring party in 2005 and was selected in the England squad for the 2007 Rugby World Cup, as he and Ben Kay formed a vital part of the side that reached the Final.

There was still more to come. In 2009, on his third tour, he finally made a Test appearance for the Lions, starting the second Test in South Africa. His performance was one of the greatest by a Lions second row in history, Shaw winning Man of the Match in what was, sadly, a losing cause.

Two years on, he made another Rugby World Cup appearance for England before bringing the curtain down on his international career.

ENGLAND STATISTICS

February 1997 – August 2003

England appearances:	51
England points:	75 (15 tries)
Lions tours:	1997, 2001

AUSTIN HEALEY

One of England's most versatile players, "The Leicester Lip" pulled on the famous white shirt more than 50 times, turning out for his country at scrum-half, fly-half and on the wing.

There are few England players who can rival Austin Healey when it comes to creativity and speed. Likewise there are few England players who can rival Healey when it comes to being outspoken and forthright. There's a reason why he is dubbed "The Leicester Lip".

In fact, Healey's personality very much represented his style of play. Constantly looking for small gaps to snipe and never willing to back down, the back became a crucial part of England's plans.

It was in 1997 that Healy got his first taste of international rugby, making his debut in the Five Nations against Ireland. That same year he earned a call-up for the Lions' tour of South Africa, where he made two appearances as a replacement in the second and third Tests. His star was rising.

At club level, Healy was quickly becoming a Leicester legend. Back-to-back Heineken Cups arrived in 2001 and 2002, with Healey playing a pivotal role. In the 2001 Final against Stade Français, it was his break that led to the winning try being scored by Leon Lloyd in a 34–30 win. A year later, Healey turned from provider to scorer as he went over the whitewash in the 59th minute during the 15–9 victory over Munster.

Healey's club form coincided with a boom in his England career, and after returning from the 2001 Lions tour of Australia he played every game until he was rested for the 2002 summer trip of Argentina.

Healey's versatility was on full display as he turned out at scrum-half, full-back and wing during England's autumn international victories in 2002.

Sir Clive Woodward then brought the curtain down on Healey's England career by deciding not to take him to the 2003 Rugby World Cup. He has later called that decision – which also included the decision not to take Simon Shaw or Graham Rowntree – the hardest of his career.

Another Lions call-up followed again in 2005, although he failed to make the final touring party.

Yet despite those disappointments, Healey goes down as one of the most exciting and attacking players to represent England.

ENGLAND STATISTICS
February 1997 – June 2004
England appearances: 71
England points: 60 (12 tries)
Rugby World Cup
winner: 2003
Grand Slam winner: 2003
Lions tours: 1997, 2001, 2005

RICHARD HILL

England's "Silent Assassin" was a fearless flanker who was a vital part of England's 2003 Rugby World Cup victory as he formed a formidable back row alongside Neil Back and Lawrence Dallaglio.

Searching for the perfect England side, Sir Clive Woodward dropped every member of his team at least once – with the exception of Richard Hill.

When fit, the flanker was guaranteed a starting spot due to his big hits and excellence at the breakdown, where he was a constant source of ball for his team – and a nuisance for the opposition.

The manner in which Woodward counted on Hill was best demonstrated at the 2003 Rugby World Cup. On the eve of the tournament, Hill suffered a hamstring injury that rendered his participation in serious doubt. Knowing he would be unable to play in any of England's Pool Games, Woodward had such faith in Hill he retained him in his squad anyway, but the flanker was still unable to play by the time of the quarter-final against Wales.

Once the team had successfully negotiated that hurdle, Hill came in for the semi-final against France and the Final against Australia. It was a sign of his enduring class and fitness that he managed to play well into extra time against the Wallabies, having dealt with a lauded French back row rather comfortably in the last four.

So it was that England lifted the Rugby World Cup in large part due to the perfect combination of their back row. With Dallaglio the ball carrier, Hill the tackler and Back the poacher, Woodward had the perfect blend. They were named the Holy Trinity, and with good reason.

Described by some as the cement between the bricks that keeps a side together, Hill made his England debut against Scotland in 1997. A one-club man, the Saracen featured throughout England's 1999 Rugby World Cup campaign and as England made their statements of intent leading into the 2003 Rugby World Cup, then winning the Grand Slam and vanquishing New Zealand and Australia in Wellington and Melbourne, respectively.

Hill also played in five Lions tests over three tours, including the victorious visit to South Africa in 1997. He brought the curtain down on his international career with the Lions in 2005 and hung up his boots three years later, his status as a legend of the game secure.

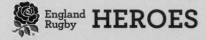

RICHARD COCKERILL

A Leicester legend who refused to back down from any confrontation, Richard Cockerill forced his way into Sir Clive Woodward's plans for the 1999 Rugby World Cup.

The haka stirs emotions and gets the blood pumping before any New Zealand international, and it certainly served to inspire Richard Cockerill.

The date was 22 November 1997 and the place was Old Trafford. Cockerill was making just his second start for England as he looked to cement his place in the side, and he decided he was going to make a statement of intent.

The haka began, and Cockerill found himself facing his opposite number, Norm Hewitt. "I thought, I'm going to find Norm, stand opposite him and then 'Come on mate, let's have a go'," Cockerill has recalled since. That he certainly did, standing just inches away from Hewitt to accept the challenge laid down by the haka.

"The Maori boys were fine with it," added Cockerill. "That's their culture – they're very big, strong, confrontational, physical people. It's a war dance, after all. It's a challenge."

It was an iconic moment – though perhaps not such an iconic afternoon, as the All Blacks won 25–8. Yet it summed up Cockerill's approach. A member of Leicester's notorious ABC Club, the hooker was a physical player who refused to take a step back.

That approach ensured he was a popular member of Sir Clive Woodward's early squads, scoring his first try for England in the win over Ireland during the 1998 Five Nations. Cockerill faced intense competition for the starting jersey from Phil Greening, among others, and Woodward began to favour his rival as the 1999 Rugby World Cup came into view.

Cockerill started every game of that year's Five Nations, but was only chosen to start in the Pool games against Italy and New Zealand during that year's Rugby World Cup. He also featured from the bench against Tonga and Fiji, but that was to be his final international appearance.

Instead he focused on Leicester and now, as the Director of Rugby at Welford Road, he plays a key role in bringing through the next generation of young English talent.

ENGLAND STATISTICS
May 1997 – October 1999
England appearances: 27
England points: 15 (3 tries)

ENGLAND STATISTICS

May 1997 – October 2007

England appearances: 64
England points: 30 (6 tries)
Rugby World Cup
winner: 2003
Lions tours: 2001, 2005

MARTIN CORRY

In more than a decade at the coalface of international rugby, Martin Corry played in three Rugby World Cups and went on to captain both England and the British & Irish Lions during an illustrious career.

If you were in any doubt over Martin Corry's commitment to the England cause, you need only look at his efforts during the 2003 and 2007 Rugby World Cups. For this most combative of forwards, they were very different experiences, but both proved his worth.

His versatility – he was equally comfortable at lock or the back row – guaranteed his place in Sir Clive Woodward's squad in 2003, but he had a dilemma: his wife was due to give birth to their first child during the tournament. There are few more gruelling journeys than that between Australia and England, but Corry decided to do a full round-the-world trip – a small matter of 21,000 miles – to witness the birth and then return in time to make his Rugby World Cup bow against Uruguay in England's glorious run to victory.

Four years later, he was a fixture in the starting line-up, making the No. 6 shirt his own. He captained the side during the Pool Stages and was a vital cog in the forward machine that drove Brian Ashton's side to the Rugby World Cup Final, where they lost to South Africa.

That was to be his final international appearance, although he played on for another two years in the colours of Leicester Tigers.

Corry's career was astonishingly successful in terms of silverware. He won five Premiership titles, two Heineken Cups and an Anglo-Welsh Cup, his move from Bristol to Welford Road in 1997 proving to be very much the right decision.

His England debut came that same year, and he played in four games during the 1999 Rugby World Cup.

Called up as a replacement for the 2001 Lions tour of Australia, he immediately made his mark and featured in all three Tests.

Four years later he was named vice-captain, and after skipper Brian O'Driscoll was injured in just the second minute of the opening Test against the All Blacks he went on to captain the side, playing in the remaining two Tests as well as the game against Argentina that opened the tour.

The same year he was named England captain, continuing in the role through the 2006 Six Nations. Then came 2007 and the chance to leave the stage in style.

ENGLAND STATISTICS
June 1997 – February 2007
England appearances: 69
England points: 10 (2 tries)
Rugby World Cup
winner: 2003
Grand Slam winner: 2003
Lions tours: 2001, 2005

DANNY GREWCOCK

Twice selected for the Lions, Danny Grewcock played 69 times for England and developed into a formidable forward for club and country.

In his day, there were few second rows who could compete with the might and prowess of Danny Grewcock. Imperious in the lineout and dangerous in the loose, the second row missed out on shining at Rugby World Cups only due to injury and suspension.

A fine partner to Martin Johnson in the powerhouse of the scrum, Grewcock had the talent to fill the great captain's boots after his retirement in 2003.

His international career had begun six years previously, against Argentina. That tour proved to be the start of a long spell in the England setup for Grewcock, and in 2001 he rose to prominence once again.

Selected for the Lions tour to Australia, Grewcock would partner captain Johnson in the second row for all three Tests. And the Bath man more than matched his partner, shining in the forwards. The Lions fell to a 2–1 series defeat, but Grewcock's stock had grown considerably. Many believed they were now looking at England's second row for the Rugby World Cup in two years.

However, Grewcock's return Down Under for the Rugby World Cup was dogged by injury. He made just one appearance in the tournament after breaking a hand against Uruguay. This meant that the second row missed out on his country's finest hour, although he was finally awarded his medal in December 2004.

After England's triumph in Australia, the void left by Johnson was clear for all to see, but Grewcock proudly stepped up to the mark. The second row was imperious in the 2004 Six Nations, earning plaudits for his brilliant displays, despite England's third-placed finish.

Grewcock went on to start all three of the Autumn Internationals that year, before once again being called up to the Lions for the 2005 tour of New Zealand. But his lack of discipline cost him through suspension a spot on the plane to the 2007 Rugby World Cup, and the second row's international career came to an end after a fine 10 years of service.

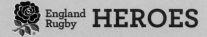

WILL GREENWOOD

Second in the all-time list of England's top try scorers, centre Will Greenwood was the brains behind his country's on-field operations and had a habit of scoring when a try was needed most.

The fact that Greenwood racked up 31 tries in just 55 appearances for England tells you all you need to know about this centre. He was a brilliant finisher, one of those players who always seemed to find a way to the line, often at the most pivotal of moments.

But there was far more to him than that. He was often credited with having the sharpest brain in rugby, speed of thought and deed more than making up for a relative lack of pace.

Rugby was in the blood for Greenwood. His father, Dick, played on the flank for England between 1966 and 1969, going on to coach the side.

His son was a promising young centre when he was thrust into the limelight by Sir Ian McGeechan, who picked him for the 1997 Lions tour to South Africa despite the fact he had yet to make his England debut.

Greenwood's tour was marred by a serious collision in which he swallowed his tongue, but he bounced back to debut for England against Australia at Twickenham that November. From that point on, he was an integral part of England's domination under Sir Clive Woodward – who once said that he and Brian O'Driscoll would have been the perfect centre pairing. One highlight was his hat-trick against Wales at the Millennium Stadium in 2001 during a run of seven tries in five games.

Acting as a big brother to Jonny Wilkinson when the fly-half first came into the team, he formed a superb 10–12–13 axis with Wilkinson and Mike Tindall, which took England to glory in 2003.

Greenwood scored five times in that tournament, including in the quarter-final against Wales.

After that triumphant 2003, Greenwood was made vice-captain to the new skipper Lawrence Dallaglio and he played all of England's Six Nations games in 2004. But England could only muster a third-place finish as Greenwood's career slowly came to a close.

He made a final appearance in the famous white jersey against Australia in November of that year, bowing out from international rugby with a final tour with the Lions to New Zealand.

"For a Blackburn lad who was only ever after a run-around with the lads, rugby has taken me on one hell of a journey," he said at the time. A true legend.

ENGLAND STATISTICS
November 1997 – November 2004
England appearances: 55
England points: 155 (31 tries)
Rugby World Cup
winner: 2003
Grand Slam winner: 2003
Lions tours: 1997, 2001, 2005

ENGLAND STATISTICS
February 1998 – March 2009
England appearances: 73
England points: 10 (2 tries)
Rugby World Cup
winner: 2003
Lions tours: 2001, 2009

PHIL VICKERY

England's "Raging Bull" was his country's premier tighthead prop for more than a decade, playing in three Rugby World Cups and captaining England on 15 occasions.

You wouldn't want to mess with England's "Raging Bull". Off the pitch he may have been one of the nicest men you could wish to meet, but on it his colossal presence made him an intimidating and formidable opponent.

Vickery was tipped to star at a young age, and certainly lived up to his billing.

This proud Cornishman made his England debut in 1998, just 34 matches into his senior career, and he was virtually ever-present in the side from then on. He played in every game during England's 1999 Rugby World Cup campaign and two years on was selected for the Lions, playing in all three Tests.

Vickery is now regarded as one of the finest props in the game, and his place in the side was unquestioned as England approached the 2003 Rugby World Cup. He had captained his country for the first time the year before on the summer tour of South America, and was one of the foundation stones on which Sir Clive Woodward's side was built.

Vickery played in every game of that stunning tournament, captaining England against Uruguay and scoring his first international try against Samoa.

His contribution was invaluable, and writing in his column for the *Daily Telegraph*, Brian Moore summed up how it felt to prepare to face Vickery. "What do you do when the man with whom you are about to lock in mortal combat, has an oriental tattoo which translated means 'I'll fight you to the death' and when you know he is a qualified cattle inseminator? You feel nervous."

Victory was sweet, but Vickery was far from finished with rugby. After recovering from serious injury, he was appointed captain ahead of the 2007 Rugby World Cup.

It was an inspired choice, as his quiet brand of leadership proved integral to England recovering from a poor start to the tournament to reach the Final. He, Ben Kay, Jason Robinson and Jonny Wilkinson were the only players to start both the 2003 and 2007 Finals.

Vickery signed off from international rugby with another Lions tour, in 2009. He retired from rugby a year later, this particular Raging Bull having been a vital part of England's success in two Rugby World Cups.

JONNY WILKINSON

The man whose drop goal was heard around the world as he kicked England to Rugby World Cup glory, Jonny Wilkinson will forever be celerbated as a hero.

If you want to know how highly Jonny Wilkinson was regarded both within rugby and by the general public, you only have to look at the tidal wave of tributes that came his way when the fly-half retired from the game in 2014.

As he prepared for retirement, it became clear quite how much he was loved and respected – not just for his playing ability, but for his professionalism, modesty and sportsmanship. He went out in glorious style, guiding Toulon to a Heineken Cup and Top 14 double as his final season.

Toulon played in shirts that had "Merci Jonny" stitched into the collars, and there was even talk of retiring the No. 10 shirt in his honour. Dan Carter, the great All Black fly-half, sent a personal message in which he revealed that his nephew copied Wilkinson's kicking style rather than his own.

What ultimately became clear is that Wilkinson has left an enduring legacy and a huge mark on the game that gave him so much. It is impossible to tell how many children have been inspired to take up the sport after watching him play, but

there have been few finer specimens in any sport than Jonathan Peter Wilkinson.

His international career began against Ireland in 1998, when he made his debut, at the age of just 18 years and 314 days, the second youngest player in English rugby history.

He became England's record points scorer in 2001, surpassing the tally of 396 held by his mentor, Rob Andrew.

But all roads were leading to 2003 by this point, and Wilkinson lived up to his billing in quite glorious style.

It is hard to exaggerate the pressure he was under when he kicked that drop goal in the final seconds of extra time during the Final against Australia, but the technique – on his weaker right foot – was simply jaw-dropping. It was the most dramatic moment in rugby history, and cemented his place as a legend of the game and a hero to millions.

Injuries bedevilled him after that, but he returned to guide England to the 2007 Rugby World Cup Final and retired from international rugby after playing in his third Rugby World Cup four years later. He did so with a tally of 1,246 Test points, a total that is unlikely ever to be beaten.

Jonny Wilkinson's Rugby World Cup-winning coach Sir Clive Woodward says of the record-breaking fly-half: "I consider myself really lucky to have had him as a player ... People talk about a model professional; well, he was the model model. He was just a great guy who worked so hard ... He was immense in every way."

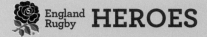

JOSH LEWSEY

With 22 tries in 55 appearances for England, Josh Lewsey was regarded as one of his country's most natural finishers and was a key man in both the 2003 and 2007 Rugby World Cups.

A moment that helped to mark the transition between rugby's amateur days and professionalism came when Sir Clive Woodward asked Josh Lewsey to remove his top during the tour to Australia in 1998.

Lewsey, just 21 at the time, did as he was told. With Lewsey's superior physical conditioning there for all to see, Woodward told the remainder of the England team, "That is what you all have to look like."

This was an approach that underpinned his illustrious international career. After missing out on the 1999 Rugby World Cup, Lewsey concentrated on his army career, graduating from Sandhurst and serving for two years as an officer with the Royal Artillery.

Returning to the international fold for the 2001 tour of North America, the full-back made his Twickenham debut only in his seventh Test, against Italy in March 2003 – a game in which he scored twice. From that point on, he was impossible to shift from the side, with Jason Robinson moving to the wing to accommodate him.

Physicality was a big weapon in Lewsey's armoury, and he made a huge statement of intent for the entire team in the victory against Australia in Melbourne before the 2003 Rugby World Cup. Wallaby Mat Rogers had been making a nuisance of himself all game, and when Lewsey was presented with a chance to make a big hit in the final minute he didn't disappoint, executing a technically perfect but brutal tackle that took the wind not just out of Rogers but the entire Australian side.

Lewsey maintained his fine form through the Rugby World Cup, scoring five times against Uruguay in the Pool Stages and starting in both the semi-final and Final.

He made an equally important impact in the 2007 World Cup. His try after just 78 seconds against France in the semi-final proved crucial, helping England reach the Final – a game he would sadly miss due to injury.

A Lion in 2005, Lewsey retired from international rugby in 2008 and indulged his passion for adventure, coming within 150m of summiting Everest.

He is currently the Welsh Rugby Union's head of rugby – although no one asks him to take his shirt off any more.

ENGLAND STATISTICS
June 1998 – October 2007
England appearances: 55
England points: 110 (22 tries)
Rugby World Cup
winner: 2003
Grand Slam winner: 2003
Lions tours: 2005

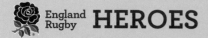
JOE WORSLEY

One of the finest tacklers in the game, Joe Worsley played in three Rugby World Cups during a 12-year international career that saw him play 78 games in the back row.

It is fitting that one of Joe Worsley's finest moments in an England shirt is a tackle. Superb in the loose and with ball in hand, the Wasps man became known throughout rugby for his fearsome tackling, with technique and aggression combining to devastating effect.

Jamie Roberts certainly has reason to remember Worsley, having been targeted by the England flanker whenever the two faced each other.

Worsley's finest moment, though, came in the Rugby World Cup semi-final of 2007. This was the tightest of games, England leading France by a point with 12 minutes to play. The ball was kicked to the wing, and France's No. 8 Julien Bonnaire tapped it down to wing Vincent Clerc. It seemed for all the world that Clerc would speed to the line, but at the last second Worsley threw himself at the Frenchman, executing the perfect ankle tap to save a certain try and take England into the Final.

"That was the turning point," said French coach Bernard Laporte afterwards. "If we had scored, the game would have been over and we would be in the Final."

"I was over the moon I could help out and make a difference," said Worsley. "I had to get on my bike to catch him. He would have won any foot race, so my only chance was to knock him off balance. I just dived and got a bit of his leg. It is what games are won and lost on."

The tackle undoubtedly won the game for England – and highlighted Worsley's contribution to the team.

It was his third Rugby World Cup: he had made his international debut during the 1999 tournament and was a squad member in 2003, playing in three games during the tournament.

His playing time increased following the retirement of Lawrence Dallaglio, but 27 of his eventual 78 appearances came from the bench.

In 2009, he was a Lion, and started the third Test victory over South Africa. Injury forced him to retire from the game in 2011, however, meaning he missed out on the chance of playing in a fourth Rugby World Cup, but his standing within the game was sky-high, according to Dallaglio. "When I think of Joe playing, my first image is always of him stopping huge South Africa forwards in their tracks all afternoon.

"I can think of very few players who are held in higher regard around the circuit. He is one of the first names you would want on the team sheet."

ENGLAND STATISTICS
October 1999 – February 2011
England appearances: 78
England points: 50 (10 tries)
Rugby World Cup
winner: 2003
Grand Slam winner: 2003
Lions tours: 2009

ENGLAND STATISTICS
February 2000 – October 2011
England appearances: 75
England points: 74 (14 tries, 2 conversions)

Rugby World Cup
winner: 2003
Grand Slam winner: 2003

MIKE TINDALL

A Rugby World Cup winner in 2003, Mike Tindall captained his country during the tournament eight years later as he won the last of his 75 England appearances.

Some players are at home on the grandest of stages, and Mike Tindall was certainly at home in the tunnel of the Telstra Stadium in Sydney before the 2003 Rugby World Cup Final.

Glancing around, the centre could see opposition stars Stirling Mortlock and Elton Flatley looking nervous. His response broke the mood perfectly. "Fellas, this is why we play rugby, isn't it? Let's get it on."

It laid the stage for a final to remember: tight, tough and settled only in the final moments of extra time.

Tindall also provided one of the moments to remember, the type of tackle that can shift the momentum and alter the course of a game. George Gregan was not a man to be messed with, but Tindall had a significant size advantage over the wonderful Wallaby scrum-half. So when the opportunity arose, he hit him well, showing superb technique to dump him on his back to loud cheers from the travelling England support.

Tindall had formed a fine centre partnership with Will Greenwood heading into the Rugby World Cup, scoring in five of his seven games going into the tournament. That included a vital try in the win over Australia in Melbourne, which many feel helped set the stage for that memorable triumph in Sydney. Tindall and Greenwood allied brains with brawn to devastating effect.

Mike Catt's kicking game was required for the semi-final against France, but Tindall fought his way back into the team for the Final as England climbed to the summit of world rugby.

He endured a torrid time with injuries after that success, missing the 2007 tournament due to a broken leg.

In 2008 he showed great courage to return from a perforated liver suffered against Wales, which left him feeling "lucky to be alive". He was a key part of the England squad for the 2011 Rugby World Cup, captaining the side in the absence of the injured Lewis Moody. Unfortunately the tournament did not pan out as either Tindall or England hoped, and he retired from international rugby after the quarter-final defeat to France.

But he, and England, will always have Sydney to remember.

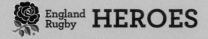

JULIAN WHITE

One of the most aggressive and powerful scrummagers in English rugby history, Julian White was a member of the World Cup-winning squad of 2003.

If you want to know how Julian White was viewed by his peers, you only have to look at the response from Lewis Moody to a tweet put out by *Rugby World magazine*. The question was: "Who is the hardest player in rugby history?" "Julian White" was Moody's immediate answer, and few would disagree.

Certainly it would be difficult to come to any other conclusion if you had ever faced the prop at the sharp end of a scrum or in the loose as he tried to get his point across. A man who was built to scrummage, White was a regular on the scene for England between 2000 and 2007, and was selected for the 2003 Rugby World Cup squad as a result.

But then his international career ground to a halt, the prop deciding he would not be available for the 2007 tournament – in part, because of work he had to do on his farm.

So it seemed he would be stuck just short of 50 appearances, a milestone any player would love to reach. Then, in 2009, he was recalled by his former Leicester team-mate Martin Johnson to play in seven more matches, and he finished his international career on 51 appearances.

It was a fine end to a career that had begun with spells playing for Hawke's Bay and the Crusaders in New Zealand, as well as Bridgend. Moves to Saracens and Bristol followed, but it was his time at Leicester for which he will primarily be remembered.

He made his England debut in 2000 and three of his first four international appearances were against South Africa. He stood up well to the Springbok test and started against France during England's Six Nations Grand Slam in 2003.

His place in Sir Clive Woodward's squad for the Rugby World Cup was secure, although Phil Vickery was first choice. White played in the games against Samoa and Uruguay as England triumphed.

But Woodward was always a fan – so much so that he selected White to start all three Tests for the Lions against New Zealand in 2005.

And the fact that White returned to reach his half-century milestone made for a fitting finale.

ENGLAND STATISTICS
June 2000 – June 2009
England appearances: 51
England points: 0
Rugby World Cup
winner: 2003
Grand Slam winner: 2003
Lions tours: 2005

ENGLAND STATISTICS
February 2001 – October 2007
England appearances: 51
England points: 140 (28 tries)
Rugby World Cup
winner: 2003
Grand Slam winner: 2003
Lions tours: 2001, 2005

JASON ROBINSON

"Billy Whizz" is one of the finest players in both union and league history, scoring England's only try in the 2003 Rugby World Cup Final on the way to becoming an England and Lions legend.

No one else has achieved what Jason Robinson has. No one else has dominated rugby league and then come to union and done the same. No one else is a Great Britain legend, an England legend (in two codes) and a Lions legend.

"Billy Whizz" was simply the most remarkable player, an individual who broke the mould, one of the most exciting talents in rugby history.

"When I look back and look at the stats, World Cups, Lions tours and Challenge Cups, I can certainly look back with some fantastic memories," said Robinson when he finally hung up those jet-heeled boots. "I have ticked almost every box there is to tick."

He certainly had. His list of achievements is extraordinary. From league superstar to union great, Robinson came through the ranks at Wigan, before switching in 2000 to Sale and the 15-man game.

Where others had failed, he thrived, and the flyer was playing for England against Italy a year later. So smooth was the transition, in fact, that he started all three Tests for the Lions in Australia that summer. Announcing himself on the world stage, he danced past Australian full-back Chris Latham to score a stunning solo try.

Australia would come to have reason to fear him again two years later. He was switched to the wing for the 2003 Rugby World Cup to accommodate Josh Lewsey, and in the quarter-final against Wales his break to set up Will Greenwood's score was decisive.

Then came his big moment against Australia in the Final. The image of Robinson punching the ball away in celebration after scoring in the corner has become almost as iconic as Wilkinson's drop goal later in the game, and meant that after just three years in the sport his place in history was secure.

Robinson wasn't done there, though. His hat-trick against Italy in his first international after the Rugby World Cup was outstanding, and despite retiring from international rugby in 2005 he was tempted back two years later.

Two tries against Scotland showed this was the right decision, and his experience was vital as England reached the Rugby World Cup Final again in 2007 – a match that really was the end of his time in an England jersey.

His was one of the great careers, and England were lucky to have him.

The Australians couldn't contain Jason Robinson during the 2003 Rugby World Cup Final and few rugby teams have been able to. Jason Robinson's Sale team-mate Steve Hanley says, "Quite simply, Jason is the best player to have ever played rugby."

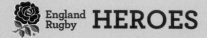

STEVE BORTHWICK

Holder of the record for Premiership appearances and master of the lineout, Borthwick earned over 50 appearances for his country while also taking over the captain's armband in 2008.

When Steve Borthwick hung up his boots at the age of 34 in 2014, it seemed that few would notice. Electing to retire at the same time as Jonny Wilkinson and Brian O'Driscoll meant that attention naturally turned to the dynamic duo, two of the game's biggest superstars.

But there are many who believe Borthwick deserved to be in such company as a master of the unseen work, the time spent at the coalface and the harsh realities of professional rugby.

Certainly Borthwick's last coach, Saracens boss Mark McCall, insists that the second-row forward deserves to be considered in a similar light to the impressive backs who have also called it quits. "[He finished as]the record Premiership appearance holder, more than 50 caps for England: he's squeezed every ounce out of his body over a 16-year period," said McCall after a season in which Borthwick led his side to both the Heineken Cup and Aviva Premiership Finals.

Similar respect came from his fellow professionals, who were well aware of the qualities Borthwick brought to England, Bath and Saracens.

Borthwick first began to assert himself on the international stage in 2004, starting every game of the Autumn Internationals. He repeated his achievement the following year, and the second row also played all of England's matches during the 2006 Six Nations.

Superb in the lineout and an inspirational leader on the field, Borthwick was maturing into a second-row forward of the highest quality. Injury hampered his continued development, leaving him to be used largely as a substitute during the 2007 Rugby World Cup. But the start of 2008 saw the second-row forward's fortunes turn once again.

He played every minute of the 2008 Six Nations as England finished runners-up, filling in as captain against Italy after Phil Vickery fell ill. In May, Borthwick was named captain for the summer tour of New Zealand and he went on to lead England for two years. Often found hunched over a laptop looking at the intricacies of the lineout, his 57 appearances for England were reason enough for him to be remembered as one of his country's finest locks.

ENGLAND STATISTICS
April 2001 – March 2010
England appearances: 57
Points: 10 (2 tries)

ENGLAND STATISTICS
June 2001 – June 2009
England appearances: 62
England points: 10 (2 tries)
Rugby World Cup
winner: 2003
Grand Slam winner: 2003
Lions tours: 2005

BEN KAY

A superb lock who was a master of the lineout, Ben Kay played a vital role in England's 2003 and 2007 Rugby World Cup campaigns.

The most games you can play in a Rugby World Cup is seven – or 560 minutes of action. To understand just how vital Ben Kay was to England in 2003 and 2007, this one stat says it all: he played a grand total of 1,060 minutes over those two tournaments.

To call him a mainstay of those two sides would be an understatement. The only game he missed in either Rugby World Cup was the Pool match against Uruguay in 2003 – apart from that, he was ever-present.

Integral to both those England sides, Kay – now a respected pundit – does still admit that some remember him more for dropping the ball in the 2003 Final with the line in sight.

"We all make mistakes," Kay laughed, later. "I just chose the biggest match of all to drop the thing! Besides, I'm pretty sure it may have been slightly forward. Overall, I was happy that I kept myself together to play a full part and to help England to a great triumph."

That he did, forming a fine second-row partnership with skipper Martin Johnson – his team-mate at Leicester – as the likes of Martin Corry and Danny Grewcock were kept out of the side.

His understanding with Johnson was to prove vital for Sir Clive Woodward, who picked him to start every game of the Six Nations as England stormed to the Grand Slam.

Kay, who joined Leicester from Waterloo when he was 23, was given responsibility for the lineout, and it was something he took very seriously indeed. So seriously, in fact, that he learnt how to count in Afrikaans in order to crack South Africa's code, which was vital in the win over the Springboks in 2003.

Kay started two Tests for Woodward on the Lions' tour of 2005 but his finest moments came with England. He was one of only four players – Jonny Wilkinson, Jason Robinson and Phil Vickery being the others – to start both the 2003 and 2007 Finals.

That Final was Kay's last start for England, with a further nine appearances following from the bench. But he will always be remembered for his exploits in 2003 and 2007 when he was a mainstay of the team that won the Rugby World Cup and a leader in the side that came so close to repeating that feat.

ENGLAND STATISTICS
June 2001 – October 2011
England appearances: 71
England points: 45 (9 tries)
Rugby World Cup
winner: 2003
Grand Slam winner: 2003
Lions tours: 2005

LEWIS MOODY

A flanker who was at his happiest when flying into rucks and making bone-crunching tackles, Lewis Moody would go on to captain his country at the 2011 Rugby World Cup.

When Lewis Moody first appeared on the scene at Leicester Tigers in 1996, the 18-year-old found the formidable figures of Neil Back and Martin Corry standing in his way. Never one to shirk a challenge, the flanker knuckled down and seven years later he was on the plane to Australia for the 2003 Rugby World Cup.

Again, Moody found himself thwarted by a back row glittering with skill and class. Back, Richard Hill and Lawrence Dallaglio had enough to force anyone onto the bench, but once again Moody didn't fall away. Instead the tireless flanker made himself a pivotal player in Sir Clive Woodward's plans, playing a part in every game of the tournament. Most importantly it was Moody who won the lineout that eventually fed Jonny Wilkinson's now fabled winning drop goal.

There are few players who can come close to the level of commitment and tenacity of Moody. He is as close to a rugby warrior as you are likely to find, willing to sacrifice anything and everything for his country. Such dedication is the reason he is loved by supporters and has earned the nickname "Mad Dog".

The honours continued to flow for the flanker as he was called up to the Lions squad for the tour of New Zealand in 2005. Despite the series loss, Moody was one of the few to come out with his reputation enhanced, putting in some impressive performances. The 2007 Rugby World Cup saw even more committed displays, with Moody shining in the knockout rounds as England reached a second successive Rugby World Cup Final.

But his committed and fearless style was perilous, and following the 2007 tournament Moody spent a portion of the next four years on the sidelines. Ankle and hip surgery, a broken ankle, an eye injury and a knee ligament problem left Moody debating whether to call it quits.

However, ever the fighter, the flanker returned to captain England during the 2011 Rugby World Cup. For Martin Johnson, one of England's greatest ever captains and the Head Coach at the time, there was no debate who should skipper the side. Moody bowed out in the quarter-final, finally hanging up his boots for a deserved rest.

ENGLAND STATISTICS
February 2002 – October 2011
England appearances: 73
England points: 20 (4 tries)
Rugby World Cup
winner: 2003
Grand Slam winner: 2003
Lions tours: 2003

STEVE THOMPSON

England's most capped hooker, a Rugby World Cup winner in 2003 and a Lion two years later, Steve Thompson caused havoc with his excellent handling and powerful running in the loose.

Like many players in the victorious squad from the 2003 Rugby World Cup, Steve Thompson goes down as one of the best players to ever represent England in his position. At 1.82m, the hooker was one of the tallest hookers in the game, but his power and size made him a handful all over the park.

It was just one year prior to England's triumph Down Under that Thompson broke into Sir Clive Woodward's setup. The hooker was making waves with his performances for Northampton Saints, earning him a call-up to the England squad for the 2002 Six Nations. He did not disappoint, starting all five matches as England claimed the Triple Crown.

In the build-up to the 2003 Rugby World Cup, Thompson's importance to the side grew. He played a pivotal role as Sir Clive's side romped to the Grand Slam during the 2003 Six Nations. England then went on to defeat all of the southern hemisphere sides as they prepared to go for glory Down Under.

Thompson played his part superbly as England claimed the Rugby World Cup for the first time, the hooker featuring in all but one of the team's matches at the tournament. He was only 25, and it was assumed that England had found a hooker who would hold the shirt for many years. But a neck injury, suffered while playing for Northampton in April 2007, forced Thompson's immediate retirement from rugby. He elected to become a coach at Brive for the following season, reluctant to leave behind the game he loved.

Thompson then stunned everyone with a return to action in October 2007. A year later, he was once again in England colours, recalled to the squad by his former captain and now coach Martin Johnson. His international rejuvenation continued as he made the 2011 Rugby World Cup squad, helping England to the quarter-finals. However, the neck injury returned once again in December that year and Thompson was finally forced to call it a day.

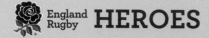

ANDREW SHERIDAN

One of the finest scrummagers ever to represent England, "Big Ted" obliterated opponents from all over the world during his 40 international appearances.

I t is safe to say there aren't, and probably never will be, many props like Andrew Sheridan. At 1.95m and weighing more than 127kg, he was one of the tallest and most formidable front-row forwards ever to take the field. Add to that the fact he could bench press 225kg and squat 275kg, and you can see why he was such a devastating player.

It was that immense power which earned Sheridan his first international cap in 2004, coming on as a replacement in England's 70–0 demolition of Canada. This was not surprising; Sheridan's talent meant he had been earmarked from an early age for an England call-up.

But the rugby world was well and truly stunned just a year later when Sir Clive Woodward selected the one-Test prop in his squad for the 2005 Lions tour of New Zealand. Admittedly Sheridan made just one appearance during the tour, but it was clear that his talents were highly regarded. People were sitting up and taking notice.

Indeed after returning from a series defeat in New Zealand, Sheridan began to showcase just

what Sir Clive had seen. In the 2005 Autumn Internationals, he dismantled the Australia scrum single-handedly. Neither of the Wallabies props finished the game, Al Baxter in the sin bin for collapsing the scrum and Matt Dunning substituted due to a neck injury. The seeds had been sown, and this would not be the last time the Aussies felt Sheridan's force.

Two years later, Australia and England met once again. This time the scene was a Rugby World Cup quarter-final, with a sunny Marseille day providing the backdrop for another Sheridan masterclass. The prop put the Wallaby scrum to the sword as England claimed a 12–10 victory thanks to four Jonny Wilkinson penalties.

Injury would go on to dog Sheridan's international career, restricting him to just 40 appearances — too small a number for such a devastating player, but he deservedly won two Lions caps on the tour of South Africa in 2009.

In September 2014 the prop announced his retirement, much to the relief of all Australian props.

ENGLAND STATISTICS
November 2004 – September 2011
England appearances: 40
England points: 0
Lions tours: 2005, 2009

ENGLAND STATISTICS
November 2006 – November 2013
England appearances: 60
England points: 301 (4 tries,
40 conversions,
66 penalties,
1 drop goal)

TOBY FLOOD

An England debutant at the age of 21, Toby Flood went on to become a key figure of the side as he strutted his stuff at fly-half and inside centre in two Rugby World Cups.

It is never easy trying to establish yourself as an England fly-half, not least when the figure of Jonny Wilkinson looms over you. But in 2006 that was exactly the task confronting Toby Flood as he made his England debut at the age of 21.

The youngster came on as a substitute against Argentina to make his international bow, but his first real test came during the 2007 Six Nations. Wilkinson had picked up an injury and Flood was chosen as the man to replace him against a France side gunning for the Grand Slam after three wins from their opening three games.

Flood stood up to the test, scoring a try as England claimed an impressive 26–18 victory at Twickenham. The fly-half made the 2007 Rugby World Cup squad, but Wilkinson's return to fitness meant he found himself playing second fiddle to the kicking maestro.

Indeed it was the Six Nations a year later which provided Flood with his chance to shine once again. This time he started at centre, with Wilkinson once again the man chosen to conduct the English back division. Flood revelled in the role, scoring two tries

during the tournament as England finished runners-up to Wales.

The tussle for the No. 10 jersey continued between Flood and Wilkinson, and by the 2010 Autumn Internationals the former was beginning to exert his dominance and live up to the early promise he had shown in his youth. Against Australia he amassed 25 points, a record for an Englishman against the Wallabies, as England cruised their way to a 35–18 win. Flood's good form continued into the Six Nations, where he was named Man of the Match in England's 26–19 win over Wales at the Millennium Stadium.

After the 2011 Rugby World Cup, Flood found his place under threat once again. Wilkinson may have gone, but the tussle for the prized No. 10 jersey was not over. A new kid was on the scene – Owen Farrell.

He started three Autumn Internationals the following year, but in 2013 he decided to bring the curtain down on his international career by moving to Toulouse.

An intelligent, clever fly-half, he succeeded in one of the hardest roles of all – succeeding Wilkinson.

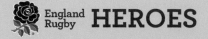

DANNY CARE

England's firecracker and a live wire around the pitch, the scrum-half has developed from a promising youngster into one of the northern hemisphere's finest halfbacks.

From an early age it was clear there was something special about Danny Care. An understudy to New Zealand scrum-half Justin Marshall at Leeds Tykes – a club where he also worked with a certain Stuart Lancaster, Care was catching the eye with his pace and innovation.

In 2005 he made the move down south, joining Harlequins. From there the scrum-half has gone from strength to strength, bringing up a half-century of appearances for England against South Africa in November 2014.

Care's first taste of Test rugby came back in 2008 against New Zealand. In terms of debuts, it doesn't come any tougher than the All Blacks in their own back yard and Care's second-half substitute was not enough to stop England going down 37–20 at Eden Park.

There were flashes of Care's youthful brilliance in that performance, though, and signs that England had a promising halfback on their hands. Indeed, Care was selected in the squads for both the 2009 and 2010 Six Nations, scoring a stunning solo try against Wales in the opening game of the 2010 tournament.

It looked as though Care had established himself as England's scrum-half, but the emergence of Ben Youngs at Leicester saw a titanic battle begin for the No. 9 shirt. Youngs usurped Care's crown in 2011 and started all five of England's Six Nations games as they claimed their first title since 2003.

Never one to lie down, Care took Youngs's presence as inspiration to drive himself on and in 2014 he demonstrated the undeniable talent he has. Youngs went into the year as a victorious Lion, having helped Warren Gatland's side topple the Australians Down Under. But Care, unperturbed, reminded Gatland and Lancaster of the ability he had with a blistering Six Nations.

The scrum-half scored the only try in England's 13–10 win over Ireland before touching down in the 29–18 win over Wales. Such was Care's confidence, he even slotted two drop goals during the tournament. England's firecracker was back with a bang.

ENGLAND STATISTICS

June 2008 – Present

England appearances:	50
England points:	44 (7 tries, 3 drop goals)

DYLAN HARTLEY

An abrasive and effective hooker who excels at the set piece and has been an integral part of the England setup under Martin Johnson and Stuart Lancaster.

When Dylan Hartley first joined Northampton Saints he was a young loosehead prop looking to make his way in the game.

Now he is recognized as one of the most accomplished hookers in the sport, a man who has mastered the set piece and brought about a level of consistency which ensures he is a regular in Stuart Lancaster's squad.

Hartley's rugby career began in earnest when he joined Worcester in 2003 after an extended holiday in England from New Zealand, where he was born and raised.

Two years later and he moved to Northampton, who quickly realized he might be more useful at the centre of the front row. It was a shrewd move, and one that has seen player, club and country reap the benefits.

Just three years after that switch Hartley was playing for England, making his debut against the Pacific Islanders at Twickenham.

Always a powerful ball carrier, Hartley's set-piece skills are vital to his game. Recognized as one of the finest lineout throwers in the game, particularly in tandem with club-mate Courtney Lawes, the Northampton captain has barely missed a match when he has been available.

Considered by many as a raw yet talented youngster when he burst on to the scene, he has developed into the most experienced member of Stuart Lancaster's squad, winning his 50th cap against New Zealand in 2013, shortly before he played his 200th match for Northampton.

A key member of Lancaster's leadership group, he captained England for the first time in the final Test of the 2012 summer tour of South Africa, a game which ended in a creditable 14-14 draw in Port Elizabeth.

Yet perhaps his finest moment in an England shirt came in 2011. Singled out by Wales coach Warren Gatland as a potential weakness beforehand, Hartley produced a stunning display as England triumphed in Cardiff.

It demonstrated his character – and is something England have had cause to be thankful for over the last seven years as he has become the third most capped hooker in his country's history.

His days as a young prop trying to find a foothold in the game seem a long time ago.

ENGLAND STATISTICS
June 2009 – Present
England appearances: 37
England points: 10 (2 tries)

CHRIS ROBSHAW

Appointed England captain in 2012 after just one appearance for his country, the flanker has developed into an inspirational leader and a brilliant back-row forward.

When Chris Robshaw was named as England's new captain ahead of the 2012 Six Nations, it would be safe to say there were a few murmurs of discontent from doubters. Despite his impressive form for the Harlequins, the flanker had last represented England two-and-a-half years previously, playing 53 minutes against Argentina.

By the end of the Six Nations, the doubters were gone and Stuart Lancaster's decision was more than justified. Under Robshaw, England romped to three away wins, including a 24–22 victory over France at the Stade de France, and only narrowly missed out on the title to Wales.

During that tournament, Robshaw played every minute and it became clear why Lancaster had chosen him as the man to lead England. The flanker typifies the new coach's ideology and style of play. A superb tackler, he has an outstanding work ethic, and his skill and speed at the breakdown go hand in hand with Lancaster's high-tempo rugby.

Robshaw's leadership qualities are hard to match too. Indeed by the end of 2014, only Martin Johnson and Will Carling had captained England on more occasions. Like many captains, he has endured some difficult periods: just as people can be quick to praise, so the critics are never far behind. But Robshaw has always risen to the challenge, particularly in 2012 against New Zealand.

The All Blacks arrived at Twickenham as World Champions, confident they could quash the English at the home of rugby. England may have enjoyed a promising Six Nations, but Robshaw's individual form was under attack.

Come the final whistle, however, England were 38–21 winners and New Zealand's 20-game unbeaten streak was over. Robshaw too had risen to the occasion, leading England forward and overcoming his opposite number Richie McCaw.

But in true Robshaw style, the tireless flanker played down the victory at the final whistle. Looking to the future, he said, "We are not going to get carried away, it's another step in the right direction."

Chris Robshaw talks to the England players at post-match huddle. Former All Black international Nick Evans says of the England captain, "He's Richie McCaw-like, in the way that he leads by example."

ENGLAND STATISTICS

Feb 2010 – Present

England appearances: 50
England points: 5 (1 try)
Lions tours: 2013

DAN COLE

A fearsome scrummager and brilliant at the breakdown, Dan Cole has developed into one of the finest tightheads in world rugby.

It was in 2010 that Dan Cole announced himself on the world stage. With club team-mate Julian White injured, Cole was called up to the England squad, making his debut at the age of 22 against Wales as a second-half substitute.

Despite his youth, Cole had made his talent clear and, after helping England to a 30–17 win, the prop went on to play in all of England's remaining Six Nations matches that year. Cole even scored his first international try in the 16–20 defeat to Ireland.

Cole's stock was rapidly growing and it was unsurprising that he was selected for England's tour of Australia that summer. Down Under, fans truly began to comprehend just how devastating a scrummager Cole could be.

England may have succumbed to a 27–17 defeat during the first Test in Perth, but the manner of their two tries showcased Cole's abilities. In unprecedented circumstances, the tighthead's scrummaging helped England secure two penalty tries, and the Wallabies' set piece was made to count for nothing. England rallied and won the next test 21–20.

From then on, Cole has become a mainstay in the England setup. Following Stuart Lancaster's appointment in 2012, Cole grew into a key component of the new coach's plans. He repaid the faith of Lancaster with another brilliant scrummaging display, this time dismantling Ireland in a convincing 30–9 win for the English.

A year later a Lions call-up followed for Cole, cementing his place as one of the finest tightheads in the northern hemisphere. The prop returned from Down Under victorious, appearing in all three of the Tests as the Lions claimed a 2–1 series win.

After that victory he was labelled by some as England's most important player, and the reaction when he suffered a serious neck injury showed just how vital he is to the England side.

Yet he slotted in like he had never been away, producing a stunning display against Wales as England won their opening game of the 2015 Six Nations.

It was yet another triumph for Cole. Often joshed by his team-mates as a dead ringer for Henry VIII, Cole really has grown into the king of the scrum for England.

INDEX

CREDITS

The publishers would like to thank the following sources for their kind permission to reproduce the pictures in this book.

Jonny Wilkinson takes the acclaim of the Sydney crowd after winning the Rugby World Cup for England in 2003.